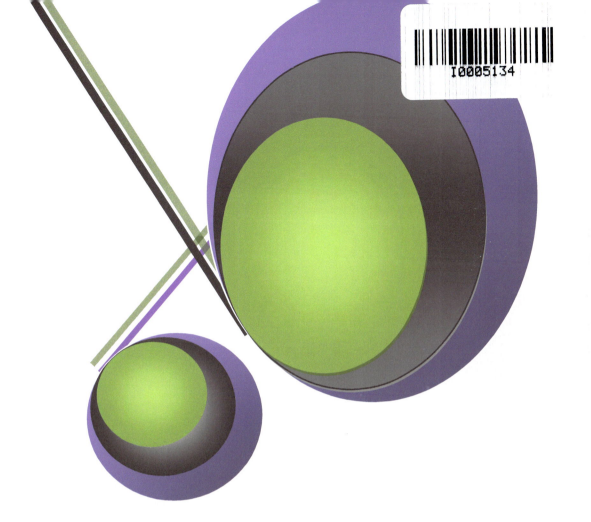

Sudhir Warier

Data Warehousing Essentials

Table of Contents

Preface 7

Acknowledgements 8

Dedication 9

Chapter 1

Data Warehousing – An Introduction 10

What is a Data Warehouse?... 13

The History of Data Warehousing 14

Data Warehousing – The Driving Forces 18

Data Warehousing – The Conceptual Basis...................... 23

Key Design Issues.. 47

Data Warehouse Tools 49

Data Warehouse Interfaces.. 52

Data Warehousing & Data Mining 53

Recommended Reading 54

Referred Standards 54

Key Terms 55

Summary 56

Check Your Learning.. 59

Knowledge Map... 63

Chapter 2

Data Modeling & Analysis 64

Introduction 69

Data Analysis Techniques 70

Data Models & Modeling Techniques 77

Data Modeling – Key Steps 86

Data Warehouse – Structure & Composition 90

Data Warehouse Architecture 100

Data Warehouse Engineering – Life Cycle 107

Recommended Reading 119

Referred Standards 120

Key Terms 120

Summary 122

Check your Learning 124

Knowledge Map 128

List of Figures 4

Notes 5

Knowledge Maps 6

Bibliography 129

Answers to Multiple Choice Questions 131

LIST OF FIGURES

Figure 1.1   Data Warehouse - Denormalization& Transformation 29

Figure 1.2   Components of a Data Warehouse 35

Figure 1.3   Data Warehouse – Key Entities 38

Figure 1.4   Data Warehouse - Contents 40

Figure 1.5   Data Warehouse – Operational Information 42

Figure 2.1   Query & Reporting Process 72

Figure 2.2   Multi Dimensional Analysis 74

Figure 2.3   Building a Data Warehouse 89

Figure 2.4   Data Warehouse – Logical Schema 94

Figure 2.5   Data Warehouse Architecture 102

Figure 2.6   Data Warehousing Life Cycle 108

NOTES

Note 1   27

Note 2   43

KNOWLEDGE MAPS

Chapter 1 63

Chapter 2 128

PREFACE

The deployment of Data Warehouses as a business application has grown tremendously over the past decade. Data warehouses are today considered to be one of the key component of an organizations overall IT strategy and architecture. This is especially true in the current Knowledge based global economy. Innovation and creativity is the current buzzword as business enterprises struggle to retain their stranglehold and find new markets for their products or services. Data warehouses are being developed and deployed for all businesses irrespective of its size and nature. They form the foundation over which the organizational Decision Support Systems are built. Foreseeing a huge growth potential major hardware and software vendors, across the world, have quickly developed products and services specifically targeting the data warehousing market. The objective of this book is to provide the reader with an insight to the world of Data Warehousing, in a lucid manner, devoid of mathematical complications.

Sudhir Warier

FIETE, MIMA, MISTD, [PhD], M.Phil, M.F.M, B.E

Acknowledgements

This book is a result of my nascent work in the field of Data Management, Warehousing and Mining systems, primarily in the framework design and system administration front. I have referred to multiple sources both print as well as online in preparing this manuscript. These may be credited for the success of this book while the failures are the result of my inadequacies. I have included references to these sources wherever appropriate. The presentation and the structure of this book is entirely my own.

In the ever-loving memory of my beloved father
C. V. M Warier

Chapter 1

Data Warehousing Essentials

Evolution, Key Components & Techniques

Objectives

The deployment of Data Warehouses as a business application has grown tremendously over the past decade. Data warehouses are today considered to be one of the key components of an organizations overall IT strategy and architecture. This is especially true in the current Knowledge based global economy. Innovation and creativity is the current buzzword as business enterprises struggle to retain their stranglehold and find new markets for their products or services. Data warehouses are being developed and deployed for all businesses irrespective of its size and nature. Foreseeing a huge growth potential major hardware and software vendors, across the world, have quickly developed products and services specifically targeting the data warehousing market. The objective of this chapter is to provide the reader with an insight to the world of Data Warehousing, in a lucid manner devoid of mathematical complications. The chapter focuses on the evolution, the organizational need and the resultant benefits in implementing a data warehousing system. The key components of a data warehousing system are also included.

KEY LEARNING'S

- Data warehousing – Evolution
- Data warehousing - Basic Concepts
- Data Warehouse Design Considerations
- Value Consistency
- Warehousing Tools – An Overview
- Data Mining – An Introduction

SUDHIR WARIER

Chapter 1

Data Warehousing – An Introduction

1.0 WHAT IS A DATA WAREHOUSE?

A Data warehouse is often mistaken as a product, or a group of products, that could be developed or purchased by an organization to supplement its decision-making capability.Data warehousing is not a product, or a set of products but a solution in itself. Data Warehousing is an information environment separate from the transaction-oriented operational environment and is evolving as a vital resource in the mordern day knowledge enterprises. A data warehouse is a part of a universal set of processes that can help an organization in its pursuit for shoring up its decision-making capabilities.   Data warehousing is the design and implementation of processes, tools, and facilities to manage and deliver absolute, opportune, accurate, and understandable information for decision-making. It includes all the activities that make it feasible for an organization to create, manage, and maintain a data warehouse.

KEY WORD
Subject Oriented Repository

A data warehouse manages data located outside the operational systems. A complete definition requires an understanding of many key attributes of a data warehouse system that are discussed in the subsequent chapters. A Data Warehouse is more than an archive and a means of storing and accessing corporate data . It is a **subject-oriented repository** designed with enterprise-wide access in mind and includes tools to satisfy the information needs of executives/managers at all organizational levels. A warehouse is not limited for complex data queries, but acts as a general facility for getting quick, accurate, and often discerning information. A Data Warehouse is designed so that its users can recognize the information they want and access that information using simple tools. A Data Warehouse is comparable to a **physical warehouse.** Operational systems create data components that are loaded into the warehouse. Some of those parts are summarized into information "components" and stored in the warehouse. Data Warehouse users make requests and are delivered information "products" that are created from the components and parts stored in the warehouse. A Data Warehouse is typically a blend of technologies, including relational and multidimensional databases, client/server architecture, extraction/transformation programs, graphical user interfaces, and more.

It is therefore not surprising that the field of data warehousing is being accorded a preferential treatment by the industry. A well-defined and properly implemented Data Warehouse can be a **valuable competitive tool** for the knowledge enabled organizations of today and the future.

1.1 THE HISTORY OF DATA WAREHOUSING

The origin of data warehousing can be linked to the commercial usage of Relational database management systems (RDBMS) in starting from the early eighties. The foundation of the relational model with its simplicity, query-handling capabilities provided by the SQL language fuelled the growth of end-user computing or **decision support systems** (DSS).

To support end-user computing environments, data is extracted from the organizational online databases and stored in newly created systems dedicated to supporting adhoc end-user queries and multiple types of reporting functions. One of the prime concerns underlying the creation of these systems is the performance impact of this resource intensive computing on the operational data processing systems. This trepidation prompted the decision to separate end-user computing systems from transactional processing systems. In the early days the data warehouse used to contain snapshots or subsets of the operational data that were updated on a regular basis. In certain cases a limited number of versions of these snapshots were accumulated in the system while access was provided to end-users equipped with standard query and reporting tools.

The underlying data models for these DSS matched the data models of the operational systems because they were extracted snapshots. The role and purpose of data warehouses in the data processing industry have evolved considerably since those early days and are still continue to evolve rapidly. Data Warehouses are no longer identified with database systems that support end-user queries and reporting functions.

Data Warehouses should no longer be conceived as snapshots of operational data but should be considered as fresh sources of information, designed for use by the whole organization or for explicit communities of users (generally smaller in size) and data analysts within the organization. The data warehousing requirements cannot be met by employing traditional data model reengineering methodologies. It calls for an applied set of modeling techniques and a much closer interaction with the business requirements of an organization.

Data warehouses consequently acts as a source of fresh information with the objective of bringing about tangible organizational benefits. The fundamental requirements of the operational and analysis systems are different: the operational systems require high performance, whereas the analysis systems need flexibility and a broader range. It is of utmost importance to ensure that business analysis does not interfere with and degrade performance of the operational systems. The following section briefly traces the different stages in the growth of data warehousing systems.

i.   **Stage 1 - Legacy Systems**

The entire system development in the early seventies was executed on IBM mainframes vide tools such as Cobol, CICS, IMS and DB2. This was followed by the deployment of mini-frame platforms such as AS/400 and VAX/VMS in the eighties, followed by the emergence of the client/server architecture. The era of distributed computing and the evolution of models to support them, starting from the early nineties, was preceded by the deployment of **UNIX** as a popular server platform. However inspite of all the changes in the platforms, architectures, tools, and technologies, a large number of business applications continue to run in the mainframe environment. This is primarily due to the fact that the applications that run on legacy systems are highly difficult to **migrate** to a new platform.

ii.   **Stage 2 - Desktop Computing**

The explosive growth of personal computing or desktop computing systems in the nineties changed the IT scenario and helped introduce many new options and compelling opportunities for business analysis. The traditional gap between the programmer and the end user diminished due to the accessibility to complex analysis and graphic representation tools. Programs facilitating the extraction and processing of information from legacy systems were designed and deployed on conventional desktop environments. However a major fallback of this model of business analysis is the problem of fragmented data (single body of data split across multiple storage locations) and its consequent personalization. This is due to the fact that each individual user obtains only the information that is required by them. This process brings introduces non-standardization and renders the extracts unusable to address the requirements of multiple users. This is a major obstacle in the development and deployment of **Knowledge Management Systems** (KMS).

iii.   **Decision-Support Systems and Executive Information Systems**

The need for efficient storage of large amounts of data has been complemented by the need for performing analysis on the stored data. **Decision Support Systems (DSS) and Executive Information Systems (EIS)** have been designed to meet the organizational information analysis requirements. Organizational analytical requirements may vary from simple operational issues to more complex decisions involving formulating business strategies. DSS are designed to focus more on details targeted to meet the operational requirements of an organization. EIS provides a higher level of consolidation and a multi-dimensional view of the data meeting the high level organizational management requirements. One of the key features of these systems is the avoidance of cryptic technical terms and their replacement by standard descriptive business terms. The data structures of these information systems are modeled to suit the usage requirements of non-technical users, thereby ensuring wider usage. The data is generally preprocessed with the application of standard business rules such as applicable to products, business units, and markets. Consolidated views of the data based on product, customer or markets can be made available. The systems can also be provided with drill down (focus) capability to uncover detail data. However the ability to simultaneously have access to all the detail data may not be present. These may be included via complex supplementary analytical tools. An important point to remember is that the success of data warehousing systems depends upon its alignment with the overall business structure rather than any specific requirements.

1.2 DATA WAREHOUSING – THE DRIVING FORCES

N O T E

📁 Key information

In the earlier days an organization with considerable financial resources could ensure its competitive advantage due to its ability to access technological advances. The growth in the field of semiconductor technology has led to the proliferation of high power computing systems at a fraction of its earlier cost, thus bring technology within the reach of the common man. The differentiating factor in the current market driven global economies lies in the deployment of technology within an organization and the harnessing of its intrinsic knowledge (knowledge within its processes, procedures, employees, vendors, data management systems…etc.)

Driven by the need to compete more effectively, corporations are leveraging the hidden value of corporate information by making it available to the widest audience of business users through two rapidly growing technology infrastructures - the Data Warehouse and the Internet. The key to success is getting users to use the information.

TECHNOLOGY ENABLERS

There are multiple factors that have influenced the quick evolution of the data warehousing discipline. The most significant set of factors has been the explosive developments in the field of semiconductor engineering and the resultant growth of hardware and software technologies. This has contributed to sharply decreasing prices and the increasing power of computer hardware. This coupled with ease of use of the currently available software, has made possible the rapid analysis of enormous quantities of information and business knowledge. The development of processors with ever increasing capabilities and feature sets along with the growth of faster and reliable storage systems, both volatile as well as non volatile, have been the major contributors toward the growth of data warehousing systems. These developments also resulted in the birth of client/server or multi-tier computing architecture systems based on the personal computers (PC), heralding the deployment of user-friendly tools providing very simple query capabilities to integrated packages providing an incredibly powerful graphical multi-dimensional analysis tools. The resultant array of choices available for data warehouse access has contributed to its rapid evolution. The emergence of server centric Network Operating Systems (NOS) such as Windows NT and the re-emergence of Unix have brought mission-critical stability and powerful features to the distributed computing environment. The abilities and the features offered by these systems have been steadily increasing while the procurement costs have been rapidly decreasing. This has led to the introduction of intricate system features including virtual memory, multi-tasking, multi-threading and symmetric multi-processing onto the desktop computing environment

The most important development in the world of computing since the advent of the PC has been the explosion of internet/intranets and web based applications.

Intranet application development has risen to become a structured and well-developed activity by itself. Intranets are private business networks that are modeled on the Internet standards. The Internet/Intranet trend has very important implications for data warehousing applications. Data warehouses can now be available worldwide on public/private network at much lower cost thus minimizing the need to replicate data across diverse geographical locations. The development of standards also facilitates the deployment of a middle tier where all the analysis takes place before it is presented to the web-browsing client for use. The increased computing power along with the availability of affordable and point-and-click reporting and analysis tools have played an important role in evolution of data warehouses.

Another key factor that has contributed to the developments in the field of data warehousing has been the development, deployment and the increasing use of business application suites by SAP AG, Baan, Oracle, PeopleSoft among other developers. This has contributes to the introduction and subsequent growth of multi-tiered application development architecture. These applications are replacing the custom developed legacy applications of yester years. These applications would be a primary data source for an organizational data warehouse. The development of standard **application programming interfaces** (API) as well as migration tools has simplified the process of porting the data from diverse organizational packages. These standard applications have extensive customization features as a result of which data acquisition from these applications can be much simpler than from the earlier mainframe systems.

ECONOMIC ENABLERS A significant influence on the evolution of the data warehousing science is the fundamental changes in the twenty-first century business organization, structure and culture. The emergence of a vibrant global knowledge based economy has had a profound impact on the information demands made by organizations worldwide. Organizations irrespective of its origins, size or sector have found markets for their products globally while competing with other business entities in vastly different cultures and economic environments. In away the economic recession witnessed across the globe in the late eighties and the early nineties contributed to the consolidation of multiple global businesses. The emergence of a global market forced organizations to reevaluate their business practices and the subsequent emergence and application of reengineering methodologies like Business Process Re-engineering (BPR). A considerable amount of effort and time were spent by organizations to identify their core competency areas and hive of non-profitable offshoots. The traditional competitive advantages enjoyed by large organizations, on account of access to the latest technological advantages, were negated by the explosive developments in the field of semiconductor technology and allied fields. This brought high end computing environments within the reach of small size businesses and the common man, thereby creating an entirely different competitive entity. Organizations had to rapidly evolve and change as per the prevailing market dynamics. These factors immensely contributed to the rapid developments in the fields of data warehousing and data mining. The banking industry has been a pioneer in the deployment and use of data warehousing technology. Organizations in India were a little slow in recognizing the potential of warehousing and mining systems, but having done so are making rapid progress in their deployment. One of the contributory factors has been the emergence of the Business Process Outsourcing (BPO) model, resulting in migration of manufacturing and the service industry to developing countries.

The modern day data warehousing systems are extensively used for increasing organizational profitability as well as customer behavior analysis. The emergence of this global economy has led to the migration of manufacturing industries to less expensive and less restrictive countries (BPO). These spurt of opportunities presented a very volatile business climate and economies that are impossible to fathom. Business enterprises have begun to focus on building of products that can sell worldwide and in the process have also changed their strategy to sell products in the emerging global markets.

This globalization of business has increased the need for a more continuous analysis and centralized management of data. The process of collating data from far-flung business units has now started to impact a larger number of corporations. **Globalization** of business has made the consolidation of data in a central data warehouse more complicated. Factors such as currency fluctuations and product customization for different markets have added complexity to data warehousing, making the analysis much more complicated.

END USER PROLIFERATION Many factors affect the heightened awareness of trends in information technology (IT) among mid and upper management levels. IT is now a universally accepted key strategic business asset and technology enabler. The explosive use of internet has greatly aided in the awareness of technology trends. The Internet is now being used to conduct business transactions; but its greatest asset to this date has been dissemination of information. Present day executives can review various industry trends and readily find case studies and vendor information online. The use of technology by mid and upper level managers has increased significantly beyond conventional email usage. This hands-on use of

SUDHIR WARIER

information and technology especially the decision making hierarchy or the top management within an organization has facilitated the sponsorship of larger projects such as data warehousing. Alongside the availability of key enabling technologies, these fundamental changes in the nature of business over the past decade have played a central role in the evolution of data warehouse.

These factors have contributed to the evolution of a technology-savvy business analyst. These technology-savvy end users play an important role in the development and deployment of data warehouses and form the core users who demonstrate the initial benefits of data warehouses. These end users are also critical to the development of the data warehouse model. Word processing and spreadsheets were the first applications to be effectively used on the PC's. The spreadsheet along with its charting functions represents one of the most extensively used business analysis and presentation functions. The new pivot tables available in popular spreadsheets have allowed for simple multi-dimensional analysis. The aggressive use of inexpensive personal productivity software has led to use of more robust reporting and analysis tools along with more powerful desktop database engines. These powerful tools are now more targeted towards the end user and often require very little training for simple applications.

1.3 DATA WAREHOUSING - THE CONCEPTUAL BASIS

Having detailed the evolution, need and the benefits of data warehousing in the preceding sections, we will now proceed to understand the basic terminologies and the conceptual basis for the design of data warehousing systems.

N O T E

📁 Key information

Based on a detailed consideration of the various attributes and functions, a data warehouse can be broadly defined on the following lines: *A data warehouse is a structured extensible environment, continuously updated and maintained for a length of time, designed for the analysis of non-volatile data [logically and physically transformed from multiple source applications] and expressed in simple business terms in alignment with the organizational business structure.*[1]

The primary concept of data warehousing is that the data stored for business analysis can most effectively be accessed by separating it from the data in the operational systems. Many of the reasons for this separation have evolved over the years. In the past, legacy systems archived data onto tapes as it became static or obsolete and many analysis reports ran from these tapes or mirror data sources to minimize the performance impact on the operational systems. These reasons to separate the operational data from analysis data have not significantly changed with the evolution of the data warehousing systems, except that now they are considered more formally during the data warehouse building process. Advances in technology and changes in the nature of business have made many of the business analysis processes much more complex and sophisticated. In addition to producing standard reports, today's data warehousing systems support very sophisticated online analysis including multi-dimensional analysis.

The most important reason for separating data for business analysis from the operational data has been the potential performance degradation on the operational system that can result from the analysis processes. High performance and quick response time is almost universally critical for operational systems.

---

1 Source: Vivek R. Gupta, An Introduction to Data Warehousing, A White paper on Data Warehousing Concepts, Source URL: < http://www.system-services.com/dwintro.asp>

The loss of efficiency and the costs incurred with slower responses on the predefined transactions are usually easy to calculate and measure On the other hand, business analysis processes in a data warehouse are difficult to predefine and they rarely need to have rigid response time requirements.

KEY ATTRIBUTES

- ✓ Data Characteristics
- ✓ Operational Terms
- ✓ Attribute definition
- ✓ Value Consistency
- ✓ Physical Model
- ✓ Logical Model
- ✓ Data Storage
- ✓ Data Transformation
- ✓ Data Summarization
- ✓ Views

For an operational system, it is typically possible to identify the mix of business transaction types in a given time frame including the peak loads. It is also relatively easy to specify the maximum acceptable response time given a specific load on the system. The cost of a high response time can be computed by considering factors such as the cost of operators, telecommunication costs, and the cost of any lost business. For example, an order processing system might specify the number of active order placed as well as the average placement per hour. Even the query and reporting transactions against the operational system are most likely to be predefined with predictable volume.

Even though many of the queries and reports that are run against a data warehouse are predefined, it is nearly impossible to accurately predict the activity against a data warehouse. It is common to have adhoc queries in a data warehouse that are triggered by unexpected results or by user's lack of understanding of the data model. Further, many of the analysis processes tend to be all encompassing whereas the operational processes are well segmented. A user may decide to explore detail data while reviewing the results of a report from the summary tables. After discovering certain interesting sales activity in a particular month, the user may explore the activity for the current month, in relation to the marketing activities conducted during the month to understand the sales pattern for a particular region. Of course, there would be instances where a user attempts to run a query that will try to build a temporary table that is a **cartesian** product of two tables containing a million rows each. While an activity like this would unacceptably degrade an operational system's performance, it is expected and planned for in a data warehousing system. Following are some of the key attributes of a data warehouse.

1. DATA CHARACTERISTICS

A key attribute of the data within a data warehouse system is that it is loaded on to the warehouse after it has become **non-volatile**. This means that after the data is in the data warehouse, there would be no modifications to be made to this information. For example: After the placement of an order, its status would not change (not the delivery status), the inventory snapshot does not change, and the marketing promotion details do not change. This attribute of the data warehouse has important implications for the kind of data that is brought to the data warehouse and the timing of the data transfer. In an operational system the data entities go through many attribute changes. For example, an order may go through many stages before it is completed, or a product flowing through a conventional assembly line would have multiple processes applied to it. In general the data from an operational system is triggered to go to the data warehouse when most of the activity on these business entity data has been completed. This may mean completion of an order or final assembly of an accepted product. Once an order is completed and shipped, it is unlikely to go back to the initial status, or once a product is developed, it is unlikely to go back to its initial production stage. Another important example can be the constantly changing data that is transferred to the data warehouse one snapshot at a time. The inventory module in an operational system may change with nearly every transaction. It is therefore impossible to carry all of these changes to the data warehouse. Depending upon the business requirements it is quite possible that a **snapshot** of inventory carried once every week to the data warehouse is adequate for all analysis. This would imply that the snapshot data is non-volatile.

Note - 1

An important point to note is that once the data is loaded onto a warehouse, it is not supposed to be modified. It is very difficult to maintain dynamic data in the warehouse. Any attempt to synchronize volatile data between operational and data warehousing systems will fail.

De-normalization

De-normalization is an important process in data warehousing modeling due to the fact that a relationship between many attributes does not change in this historical data. For example, in an operational system, a product may be part of the product group "A" in a current month and product group "B" from the subsequent month. In a properly normalized data model, it would be inappropriate to include the product group attribute with an order entity that records an order for this product; only the product ID would be included. The relational theory would stipulate a join on the order table and product table to determine the product group and any other attributes of the specified product. This relational theory concept does not apply to a data warehousing system because in a data warehousing system one may be capturing the group that this product belonged to when the order was filled. Even though the product moves to different groups over time, the relationship between the product and the group in context of this particular order is static.

Another important example can be the price of a product. The prices in an operational system may change constantly. Some of these price changes may be carried to the data warehouse with a periodic snapshot of the product price table. In a data warehousing system one would carry the list price of the product when the order is placed with each order regardless of the selling price for this order. The list price of the product may change many times in a year and the product price database snapshot may even manage to capture all these prices. But, it is nearly impossible to determine the historical list price of the product at the time each order is generated if it is not carried to the data warehouse with the order. The relational database theory makes it easy to maintain dynamic relationships between business entities, whereas a data warehouse system captures relationships between business entities at a given time. The concept of de-normalization and transformation is illustrated in the figure 1.1 below.

Figure 1.1 – Data Warehouse - Denormalization& Transformation

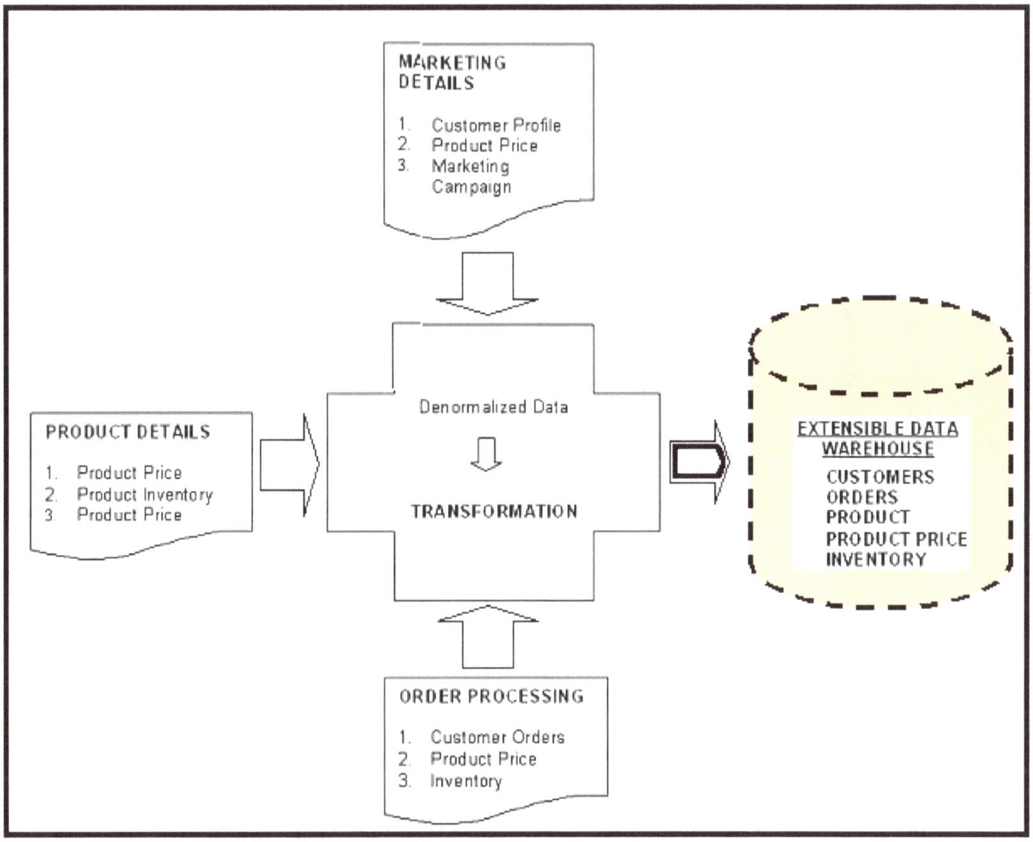

Related Topic

Data Normalization

The relational database theory was formulated in the late sixties by a researcher at IBM, E. F. Codd. Many prominent researchers have made significant contributions to this model since its introduction. Today, most of the popular database platforms follow this model closely. A relational database model is a collection of two-dimensional tables consisting of rows and columns. In the relational modeling terminology, the tables, rows, and columns are respectively called relations, attributes, and tuples. The name for relational database model is derived from the term relation for a table. The model further identifies unique keys for all tables and describes the relationship between tables.

Normalization is a relational database modeling process where the relations or tables are progressively decomposed into smaller relations to a point where all attributes in a relation are very tightly fixed with the primary key of the relation. Most data modelers try to achieve the "Third Normal Form" with all of the relations before they de-normalize for performance or other reasons. The three levels of normalization are briefly described below:

1.   **First Normal Form**

A relation is said to be in First Normal Form if it describes a single entity and it contains no arrays or repeating attributes. For example, an order table or relation with multiple line items would not be in First Normal Form because it would have repeating sets of attributes for each line item. The relational theory would call for separate tables for order and line items.

2.   **Second Normal Form**

A relation is said to be in Second Normal Form if in addition to the First Normal Form properties, all attributes are fully dependent on the primary key for the relation.

3.   **Third Normal Form**

A relation is in Third Normal Form if in addition to Second Normal Form, all non-key attributes are completely independent of each other.

The process of normalization generally breaks a table into many independent tables. While a fully normalized database can yield a flexible model, it generally makes the data model more complex and difficult to follow. The performance of a fully de-normalized database system would be very low. A data modeler in an operational system would take normalized logical data model and convert it into a physical data model that is significantly de-normalized. **De-normalization** reduces the need for database table joins in the queries.

The reasons for de-normalizing the data warehouse model are the same as they would be for an operational system, namely, performance and simplicity. The data normalization in relational databases provides considerable flexibility at the cost of the performance. This performance cost is sharply increased in a data warehousing system because the amount of data involved may be much larger. A query with relatively small tables of an operational system may be acceptable in terms of performance cost, but the same may take unacceptably long time with large tables in the data warehouse system.

2. OPERATIONAL TERMS

The terms and names used in the operational systems are transformed into uniform standard terminology by the data warehouse transformation processes. The operational application may use cryptic or difficult to understand terms for a variety of different reasons. The platform software may impose length and format restriction on a term, or purchased application may be using a term that is too generic for the business. The data warehouse needs to consistently use standard business terms that are self-explanatory.

A customer identifier in the operational systems may be called cust, cust_id, or cust_no. Further, different operational applications may use different terms to refer to the same attribute. For example, a home loan customer of a bank may be referred to as a HL_Borrower whereas a Personal Loan customer may be referred as PL_Borrower. One may choose a simple standard business term such as Customer Id in the data warehouse. This term would require little or no explanation even to a layman.

3. ATTRIBUTE DEFINITION

Different systems may evolve to use different lengths and data types for the same data element. One system may have the product ID to be either 12 or 14 numeric characters, whereas another system may accommodate product IDs of up to 18 alphanumeric characters. The software of an operational application may support very limited data types and it may impose severe limitations on the names. Software of another application may support a very rich set of data types, and it may be very flexible with the naming conventions. As an attribute is defined physically for the data warehouse, it is essential to use meaningful data types and lengths. Use the standard data length and data type for each attribute everywhere it is used. A functional data dictionary or a reference can facilitate this consistent use of physical attributes.

4. VALUE CONSISTENCY

All attributes in the data warehouse need to be consistent in the use of predefined values. Different source applications invariably use different attribute values to represent the same meaning. These different values need to be converted into a single, most sensible value as the data is loaded into the data warehouse.

A simple example for the consistent use of entity attributes is the use of a gender flag for an individual. One source application may use flags such as "M" and "F" to store gender for an individual whereas another application may use the detail "Male" and "Female" to store gender. Other applications may use yet other values to store the same piece of information. The data warehouse may choose to consistently use "M" and "F" for gender for all individuals throughout the system. A more complex example can be the case of dealing with complex data values in the source application. Many older applications use single data value to represent multiple attributes. An account number, for example, may not only represent a unique account but also it may also represent the account type. All accounts starting with 4000 may represent one type of account whereas all other accounts may represent something else to the business. The data warehouse would consistently use the account ID to only represent a unique account. The account type may be computed and saved as a separate attribute.

5. PHYSICAL MODEL

The **data warehouse model** outlines the **logical** and **physical structure** of the data warehouse. As opposed to the archived data of the legacy systems, considerable effort needs to be devoted to the data warehouse modeling. This data modeling effort in the early phases of the data-warehousing project can result in the development of an efficient data warehouse that is expandable to accommodate all of the business data from multiple operational applications, thus providing significant benefits to the organization.

The data modeling process needs to structure the data in the data warehouse independent of the relational data model that may exist in any of the operational systems. The data warehouse model is likely to be less normalized than an operational system model. Further, the operational systems are likely to have large amounts of overlapping business reference data. Information about current products is likely to be used in varying forms in many of the operational systems. The data warehouse system needs to consolidate all of the reference data. For example, the operational order processing system may maintain the pricing and physical attributes of products whereas the R&D department may maintain design and formula attributes for the same product. The data warehouse reference table for products would consolidate and maintain all attributes associated with products that are relevant for the analysis processes. Some attributes that are essential to the operational system are likely to be deemed unnecessary for the data warehouse and may not be loaded and maintained in the data warehouse.

The data warehouse model needs to be extensible and structured such that the data from different applications can be added as a business case can be made for the data. A data warehouse project in most cases cannot include data from all possible applications right from the start. Most of the successful data warehousing projects take an incremental approach to adding data from the operational systems and aligning it with the existing data. They start with the objective of eventually adding most if not all business data to the data warehouse. Keeping this long-term objective in mind, they may begin with a couple operational applications that provide the most important data for business analysis. The Figure 1.2 below illustrates the extensible architecture of the data warehouse.

Figure 1.2 – Components of a Data Warehouse [1]

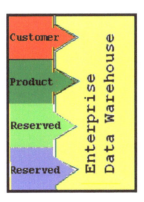

6. LOGICAL MODEL

A data warehouse logical model aligns with the business structure rather than the data model of any particular application. The entities defined and maintained in the data warehouse parallel the actual business entities such as customers, products, orders, and distributors. Different parts of an organization may have a very narrow view of a business entity such as a customer. For example, an housing loan department of a bank may only know about a customer in the context of the personal loan department. Another group in the same bank may know about the same customer in context of a recurring deposit account. The data warehouse view of the customer would transcend the view from a particular part of the business. A customer in the data warehouse would represent a bank customer that has any kind of business with the bank.

A data warehouse would most likely build attributes of a business entity by collecting data from multiple source applications. Consider, for example, the demographic data associated with a bank customer. The retail operational system may provide some attributes such as PAN number, address, and phone number. A loan system or some purchased database may provide with employment, income, and net worth information. The structure of the data in any single source application is likely to be inadequate for the data warehouse. The structure in a single application may be influenced by many factors, including:

i) **Third Party Applications**

The application data structure may be dictated by an application that was purchased from a software vendor and integrated into the business. The user of the application may have very little or no control over the data model. Some vendor applications have a very generic data model that is designed to accommodate a large number and types of businesses.

ii) Legacy Applications

The source application may be a very old proprietary application where the data model has evolved over the years. The database engine in this application may have been changed more than once without anyone taking the time to fully exploit the features of the new engine. There are many legacy applications in existence today where the data model is neither well documented nor understood by anyone currently supporting the application.

iii) Platform Limitations

The source application data model may be restricted by the limitations of the hardware/software platform or development tools and technologies. A database platform may not support certain logical relationship or there may be physical limitations on the data attributes. The following figure 1.3 depicts the alignment of the data warehouse entities with the business structure. The data warehouse model breaks away from the limitations of the source application data models and builds a flexible model that parallels the business structure. This extensible data model is easy to understand by the business analysts as well as the managers.

Figure 1.3 – Data Warehouse – Key Entities

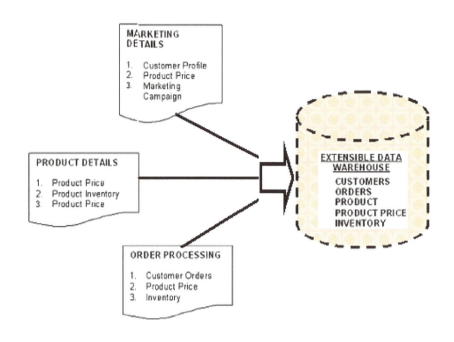

Data from most of the operational systems is archived after the data becomes inactive. For example, an order may become inactive after a set period from the fulfillment of the order, or a bank account may become inactive after it has been closed for a period of time. The primary reason for archiving the inactive data has been the performance of the operational system. Large amounts of inactive data mixed with operational live data can significantly degrade the performance of a transaction that is only processing the active data. Since the data warehouses are designed to be the archives for the operational data, the data is saved for a very long period. The cost of maintaining the data once it is loaded in the data warehouse is minimal. Most of the significant costs are incurred in data transfer and ensuring its consistency. Storing data for more than five years is very common for data warehousing systems. Normally one would start with storing the data for two or three years and then expand to five or more years once the affluence of business knowledge in the data warehouse is discovered. The falling prices of hardware have also encouraged the expansion of successful data warehousing projects.

The separation of operational data from the analysis data is the most fundamental data-warehousing concept. Not only is the data stored in a structured manner outside the operational system, businesses today are allocating considerable resources to build data warehouses at the same time that the operational applications are deployed. Rather than archiving data to a tape as an afterthought of implementing an operational system, data warehousing systems have become the primary interface for operational systems. The figure 1.4 below highlights the reasons for separation as discussed in this section.

Figure 1.4 – Data Warehouse - Contents [1]

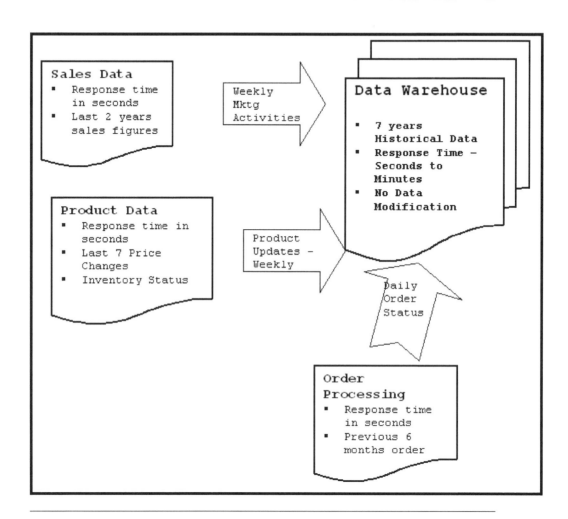

8. DATA TRANSFORMATION

The data is **logically transformed** when it is brought to the data warehouse from the operational systems. The logical transformation of the data brought from the operational systems to the data warehouse may require considerable analysis and design effort. The **architecture** of the data warehouse and the associated **data warehouse model** greatly impacts the success of an organizational warehousiing project. This section introduces some of the most fundamental concepts of relational database theory that do not fully apply to data warehousing systems. Even though most data warehouses are deployed on relational database platforms, some basic relational principles are knowingly modified when developing the logical and physical model of the data warehouses.

It is essential to understand the implications of not being able to maintain the state information of the operational system when the data is moved to the data warehouse. Many of the attributes of entities in the operational system are very dynamic and constantly modified. Many of these dynamic operational system attributes are not carried over to the data warehouse; others are static by the time they are moved to the data warehouse. A data warehouse generally does not contain information about entities that are dynamic and constantly going through state changes. The above concept is highlighted in the followiing example: An order tracking system that tracks the inventory to fill orders. An order may go through many different stages or states before it is fulfilled or goes to the "closed" status. Other order status may indicate that the order is ready to be serviced, is being serviced ready to be shipped, etc. This order entity may go through many states that capture the status of the order and the business processes that have been applied to it. It is nearly impossible to carry forward all of attributes associated with these order states to the data warehousing system. The data warehousing system is most likely to have just one final snapshot of this order. As the order is ready to be moved into the data warehouse, the information may be gathered from multiple operational entities such as order and shipping to build the final data warehouse order entity.

Figure 1.5 – Data Warehouse – Operational Information [1]

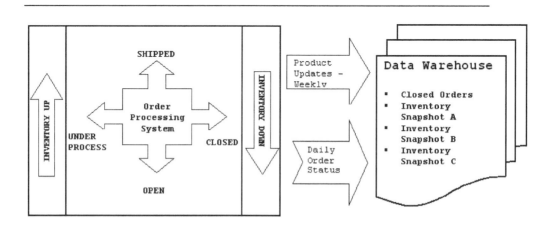

The Figure 1.5 above illustrates how most of the operational state information cannot be carried over the data warehouse system. The inventory may change with every single transaction. The quantity of a product in the inventory may be reduced by an serfviced order transaction or this quantity may be increased with receipt of a new product shipment. If this order processing system executes nine thousand transactions in a given day, it is likely that the actual inventory in the database will go through just as many states or snapshots during this day. It is impossible to capture this constant change in the database and carry it forward to the data warehouse. This is still one of the most perplexing problems with the data warehousing systems. There are many approaches to solving this problem. The most common method is to carry periodical snapshots of the inventory data to the data warehouse. This scenario can apply to a very large portion of the data in the operational systems. However this get much more complicated as extended time periods are considered.

Physical transformation of data results in its **homogenization** and **cleansing**. These data warehousing processes are typically known as "**data scrubbing**" or "**data staging**" processes. The "data scrubbing" process is one of the most time consuming and laborious processes within a warehousing project. However these processes cannot be eliminated, as it would result in the diminishing the analytical value of even the clean data. Physical transformation includes the use of simple or lucid standard business terms, and standard values for the data. A complete dictionary associated with the data warehouse can be a very useful tool. During these physical transformation processes the data is sometimes "**staged**" before it is entered into the data warehouse. The data may be combined from multiple applications during this "staging" step or the integrity of the data may be checked during this process.

Note - 2

Historical data and the current operational application data are likely to have some missing or invalid values. It is important to note that it is essential to manage missing values or incomplete transformations while moving the data to the data warehousing system. The end user of the data warehouse must have a way to learn about any missing data and the default values used by the transformation processes.

9. DATA SUMMARIZATION

Most of the queries and reports that are build in data warehouse systems are simple aggregations based on predefined parameters. Another key attribute of the data warehouses is the predefined and automatically generated summary views. For example, many people in an organization may need to see sales figures for a particular product. They may have a need to summarize these sales figures for a week, a month, or a quarter. It may not be practical to summarize the needed data every time an analyst requires it. A data warehouse that contains summary views of the detail data around the most common queries can sharply reduce the amount of processing needed at the time of analysis. Summary views are typically created around business entities such as customers, products etc.

The **summary views** also hide the complexities of the detail data. Performance gain is the most significant tangible aspect of the summary views in the data warehouse. Most relational databases provide the ability to build views for users that hide the underlying tables. In most SQL server packages, including MS SQL Server, the view exists only as a definition and it is created at the time it is actually used. While the concept of summary views in data warehousing systems is similar, it important to not confuse data warehousing summary views with the term "views" as it is used in a database system. A summary view in a data warehouse refers to an actual table that is created and maintained independent of when it used by a user.

10. VIEWS

Summary views often are generated not only by summarizing the detail data but also by applying business rules to the detail data. For example, the summary views may contain a filter that applies the exact business rules for considering an order of sale or a filter that applies the business rules for allocating a sale to a franchisee. The summary views can hide the complexities of the detail data from the end user.

The generation of summary view necessitates the application of complex business rules. These business rules may determine exactly what constitutes a sale or they may determine how a sale is allocated to a franchisee. Large organizations often have complex rules to charge sales to different franchisee accounts. Some sales may be allocated to warranty replacement and thus not be counted as sales. It is also possible that some sales may be further discounted based on a master contract with the customer and thus need to be reduced when calculating product sales for a period. A data warehouse will generally have more than one views based on business entities such as customers and products. There may be multiple physical tables or the same table may contain additional attributes that allow for easy queries.

In addition to applying the business rules while generating summary views, the data warehousing system may perform complex database operations such as **multi-table joins**. Product sales may be computed by joining the Sales, Invoice, and Product tables. The criteria to join these tables may be complex. While individuals mining data in the warehouse detail records need to understand all the complexities of business rules, most users can retrieve effective summary business information without fully understanding the detail data.

KEY ADVANTAGES

🗁 Performance Gain

The single most important reason for building the summary views is the significant performance gains they facilitate. Not only are all the complexities of detail data interpreted for an end user; the summary views also perform the most time-consuming data analysis before it is needed.

Summary views allow one to run a product sales query by merely setting up a filter based on indexed fields such as date, product codes, and other relevant criteria. The summary views will result in a query being run on a smaller table thus providing faster results and the usage of significantly reduced processing power. However in some instances a summary view table can be as large as the detail tables. This may be caused by summarization in very small units or combining multiple summary views into one data table. For example, one may not be able to summarize the product sales by week. Instead daily product sales figures may be required for some queries. Even in these large summary views, the performance is generally better because many of the table joins are eliminated and queries can generally use the indexes.

The summary views in a data warehouse provide multiple views into the same detail data. These views are predefined dimensions into the detail data. These views provide an efficient method for the analyst to link with the detail data when necessary. For example, for the sales order data, four different product sales summary views could be generated, summarizing weekly sales data. These views are summarized by product, customer, franchisee and state and include the same detail data that needs to be updated or regenerated as new data is brought into the data warehouse. Even though most of the analysis is likely to be done using the summary views, there needs to be a simple and robust way for an analyst to drill down into the detail data. Many business problems require review of the detail data to fully understand a pattern or anomaly exhibited in the summarized reports or queries. Drill down from many different summary views can lead to the same detail data. A single anomaly in detail data may manifest itself differently in different summary views.

Summarization and predefined analysis of data in a data warehouse system is an important task. It is essential to maintain the integrity of the summary views because very large parts of the data warehouse activity is against the summary views. It is important to note that the summary views needs to be maintained as new data comes into the data warehouse.

1.4 KEY DESIGN ISSUES

The data brought into the data warehouse is sometimes incomplete or contains values that cannot be transformed properly. It is very important for the data warehouse transformation process to use intelligent default values for the missing or corrupt data. It is also important to devise a mechanism for users of the data warehouse to be aware of these default values. Some data attributes can easily be defaulted to a reasonable value when the original is missing or corrupt. Other values can be obtained by referencing other current data. For example, a missing product attribute such as unit-of-measure

DESIGN ISSUES

- SUMMARY

- 🗁 Data Transformation
- 🗁 Missing Values
- 🗁 Operational System Integration
- 🗁 Value Consistency
- 🗁 Time Dimension
- 🗁 Version Integration

on an order entity can be obtained by accessing the current product database. Some attributes cannot be filled by defaults for missing values. In fact, it may be dangerous to attempt to assign default for certain types of missing values. A poor default may corrupt the data and lead to invalid analysis at a later stage. In these cases, it is safest to leave the missing values as blank. In some cases, it may make

47 | P a g e

SUDHIR WARIER

sense to pick a specific value or symbol that indicates a missing value. The timing of the start of the period for which data is loaded into the data warehouse can be important. It is safest to load data in the data warehouse for complete years.

It is important to design a good system to log and identify data that is missing from the data warehouse. When a user runs a query against the data warehouse, it is essential to understand the population against which the query is run. Physical transformation of source application data requires considerable effort and it can be difficult at times, but a well-considered set of physical data transformations can make a data warehouse user-friendlier. Further, accurate and complete transformations help maintain the integrity of the data warehouse.

Data warehousing systems are most successful when data can be combined from more than one operational system. When the data needs to be brought together from more than one source application, it is natural that this integration be done at a place independent of the source applications. A data warehouse effectively combines data from multiple source applications such as sales, marketing, finance, and production. Many large data warehouse architectures allow for the source applications to be integrated into the data warehouse incrementally. The primary reason for combining data from multiple source applications is the ability to cross-reference data from these applications. All the date within a warehouse is built around the time dimension and is the primary filtering criterion for a very large percentage of all queries against the data warehouse. An analyst may generate queries for a given week, month, quarter, or a year. Another popular query in many data warehousing applications is the review of year-on-year activity. For example, one may compare sales for the first quarter of the year 2006 with the sales for first quarter of the years 2005 and 2004. The time dimension in the data warehouse also serves as a primary cross-referencing attribute. For example, an analyst may attempt to access the impact of a new marketing campaign run during selected months by reviewing the sales during similar periods. The ability to establish and understand the correlation between activities of different organizational SBU's is one of the primary features offered by data warehousing systems.

The data warehouse system can serve not only as an effective platform to merge data from multiple current applications but can also be used to integrate multiple versions of the same application. For example, an organization may have migrated to a new standard business application that replaces a legacy application. The data warehouse system can combine the data from the old and the new applications. A properly designed data warehouse can allow for continual analysis even though the base operational application has changed.

1.5 DATA WAREHOUSE TOOLS

PRIMARY TOOLS
- Standard Reports & Queries
- Summary Table Query
- Data Mining in Detail Data

A data warehouse is designed to be highly open and flexible. The data warehouse should be accessible by as many end-user tools and platforms as possible. However it may always not be possible to make every feature of the data warehouse available from all the end user tools employed within an organization.

The simple query capability built into most spreadsheets may be adequate for a user that only needs to quickly reference the data warehouse. Other users may require the use of the most powerful multidimensional analysis tools. The data warehouse administrators need to identify the tools that are supported for access to the data warehouse and the capabilities that are available using these different tools. In most data warehousing projects, there is a need to select a preferred data warehouse access tool for the most active users. A small number of users generate most of the analysis activity against the data warehouse. The data warehouse performance can be tuned to the requirements of the tool appropriate for these active users. This tool can be used for training and demonstration of the data warehouse. The following are some of the commonly employed warehouse access tools:

STANDARD REPORTS AND QUERIES

Many users of the data warehouse need to access a set of standard reports and queries. It is desirable to periodically and automatically produce a set of standard reports that are required by many different users. When these users need a particular report, they can just view the report that has already been run by the data warehouse system rather than running it themselves. This facility can be particularly useful for reports that take a long time to run. However such facilities would require a client-server environment with the reports being accessed using the client program. This facility would need to work with or be part of the data warehouse access tool. Besides these an organization may also provide a web interface to the reports. In many data warehouse systems, this report and query server becomes an essential facility. The data warehouse users and administrators constantly need to consider any reports that are candidates to become standard reports for the data warehouse. Frequently, individual users may develop reports that can be used by other users. In addition to standard reports and queries, sometimes it is useful to share some of the advanced work done by other users. A user may produce advanced analysis that can be parameterized or otherwise adapted by other users in different parts of the same organization or even in multiple organizations.

Queries against Summary Tables

As introduced earlier, the summary views in the data warehouse can be the object of a large majority of analysis in a data warehouse. Most of the analytical activity within a warehouse is confined to simple filtering and summation from the summary views. These summary views contain predefined standard business analysis.

For example, in a typical data warehouse, the product summary view may account for a very large number of queries where different users select different products and the time periods for product sales and profit margin queries. These queries provide quick response and they are very simple to build. Advanced users typically attach a pivot table in their analysis tool to data warehouse summary tables for simple multi-dimensional analysis.

Data Mining in the Detail Data

The data mining in the detail data accounts for a very small percentage of the data warehouse activity. However the most useful organizational data analyses are done on the detail data. The reports and queries off the summary tables are adequate to answer many "what" questions in the business. The drill down into the detail data provides answers to "why" and "how" questions.

Data mining is an evolving science. A data-mining user starts with summary data and drills down into the detail data looking for arguments to prove or disprove a hypothesis. The tools for data mining are evolving rapidly to satisfy the need to understand the behavior of business units such as customers and products.

1.6 Data Warehouse Interfaces

The data warehouse system would be interfaced with other applications that use it as the source of operational system data. A data warehouse may feed data to other data warehouses or smaller data warehouses called data marts. The operational system interfaces with the data warehouse are inherently stable.   Since an organizational data warehouse is a reliable source of data that is consistently separate from the operational systems a single interface with the interfacing operational applications is much easier and more functional than multiple interfaces. The data warehouse can be a consistent source satisfying application needs for a variety of data as opposed to the operational systems. However it is important to note that much of the operational state information is moved onto a data warehouse.   Hence a data warehouse cannot be a source for all operation system interfaces. Although a majority of the activity against most data warehouses is simple reporting and analysis, higher end complex analytical functions are being rapidly developed. The analysis performed by a warehouse is much simpler and much cheaper from an organization standpoint and hence contributes significantly to its wide spread deployment.

1.7 Data Warehousing and Data Mining

A data-mining user starts with summary data and drills down into the detail data looking for arguments to prove or disprove a hypothesis. The tools for data mining are evolving rapidly to satisfy the need to understand the behavior of business units such as customers and products. Data Warehouses are intended to deliver information derived from a variety of operational systems to support the business analysis needs of an organization. While much of the challenge in building a successful data warehouse lies in its design and the transfer of data, an equally important challenge arises in the deployment of the data warehouse. Pre-defined queries and reports are typically used to satisfy routine information requirements. However in dynamic business environment users need answers to everyday business questions on an ad hoc basis. A handful of technically astute users are capable of serving themselves information with almost any tool, but reaching beyond the power user to the mainstream business user has proven to be a significant challenge. For this reason, many data warehouses have failed to meet their original goals. Deploying the data warehouse on the Internet, or on a private corporate intranet/extranet – makes the data warehouse available to anyone with a web browser. This eliminates the complexities involved in the installation and administration of data analysis (OLAP) tools on each client machine. Further it also eliminates the need to train and support users to operate all the complex OLAP tools. Targeting such a large user population requires a new and more natural way for users to interact with their computers. One of the principal reasons for developing a Data Warehouse is to integrate operational data from various sources into a single and consistent architecture that supports analysis and decision-making within the enterprise. Operational (legacy) systems create, update and delete production data that "feed" the Data Warehouse.

1.8 RECOMMENDED READING

BOOKS

1. Ponniah Paulraj, Data Modeling Fundamentals: A Practical Guide for IT Professionals, Wiley-Interscience, ISBN-13: 978-0471790495
2. Kimball Ralph & Ross Mary et.al, The Data Warehouse Toolkit: The Complete Guide to Dimensional Modeling (2nd Edition), 2008, Wiley ISBN-13: 978-0470149775
3. Inmon Bill, Building The Data Warehouse, 4th Edition, Wiley, ISBN-13-978-0764599446

URL

http://www.1keydata.com/datawarehousing/concepts.html

http://www.principlepartners.com/presentations/DataWarehouseConceptsAndArchitecture.pdf

http://en.wikipedia.org/wiki/Data_warehouse

http://www.users.qwest.net/~lauramh/resume/thorn.htm

http://www.agiledata.org/essays/dataNormalization.html

1.9 REFERRED STANDARDS

Meta Data Coalition (MDC)[i] Open Information Model

Object Management Group (OMG)[ii] Common Warehouse Metamodel (CWM)

1.10 Key Terms [nomenclature]

Business Process Outsourcing (BPO)

Business Process Re-engineering (BPR)

Cleansing

Data Mining

Data Scrubbing

Data Staging

Decision Support Systems (DSS)

De-normalization

Executive Information Systems (EIS)

Homogenization

International Business Machines (IBM)

Knowledge Management Systems (KMS)

Multi-Dimensional Analysis

Multi-table joins

Network Operating System (NOS)

Normalization

On-line Analytical Processing (OLAP)

Permanent Account Number (PAN)

Personal computers (PC)

Relational database management systems (RDBMS)

Research & Development (R&D)

Small Business Units (SBU)

Structured Query Language (SQL)

Summary views

1.11 SUMMARY

KEY BENEFITS

- 📁 Improved Decision Making
- 📁 Enhanced Customer Services
- 📁 Information Re-Engineering

Data Warehousing is a science that will continue to evolve with time. This chapter introduced the fundamental concepts of data warehousing along with its need and benefits. The concepts introduced in this chapter provide an indication of the scope an application of a data warehousing systems. The technological advances in the computing arena (both hardware as well as software) will continue to greatly influence the capabilities that are built into data warehouses. Data warehousing systems have become a key component of the organizational IT architecture.

The concept of data warehousing evolved out of the organizational need for easy access to a structured store of quality data in order to buttress its decision-making capabilities. It is a universally recognized and accepted fact that knowledge is one of the key assets that can be leveraged by organizations to provide significant benefits, including competitive advantages in the current knowledge economy. Organizations generally have stockpiles of data but find it increasingly difficult to

IMPROVED DECISION MAKING

access, analyze them and assimilate the key learning's in their day-to-day functioning. This is because of the diversity of operational platforms as well as the enormity of the various formats involved. This problem is further compounded by the storage of the data in radically diffcrent file and database structures developed by different vendors. Thus organizations thus would need to develop and employ scores of software programs to handle the extraction; processing and consolidation of the data, to meet the needs of the various analytical tools deployed leading to time and cost overruns.

Data warehousing offers a superior approach to avoid the above-mentioned problem. Data warehousing implements processes to access heterogeneous data sources with the ability to clean, filter, and transform the data while providing a structured storage mechanism, that is easy to access, understand, and use. This data can subsequently be used for querying, reporting, and data analysis. An added advantage of deploying an organizational data warehousing environment is the reduction of staff and other allied resources required to support queries and reports against operational and production databases. This brings about significant reduction in cost besides eliminating the resource drain on production systems due to the execution of time intensive complex queries. The multi-tiered data structure employed by warehouse facilitates enterprise analysis ranging from detailed transactional queries to high-level summary information, with an increased flexibility and quality resulting in better organizational decision making.

The Data Warehouse architecture helps organization foster better relationships

ENHANCED CUSTOMER SERVICES

with its customers both internal and external. This is due to resultant correlation of all customer data via a single Data Warehouse architecture. This is a very crucial aspect in any organization irrespective of its domain, size or structure, more so in service providing entities. For example a customer requiring financial services from a banking provider would not require submitting certain basic details and may be accorded additional facilities based on his past relationship with the business entity.

RE-ENGINEERING Path breaking ideas for reengineering key organizational business or allied processes may often be attributed to insightful information obtained form unlimited analysis of enterprise information. The task of defining the data warehouse requirements would also lead to the establishment of better enterprise goals and measures. Knowing what information is important to an enterprise will provide direction and priority for reengineering efforts. A Data Warehouse that is based upon enterprise-wide data requirements provides a cost-effective means of establishing both data standardization and operational system interoperability. Data Warehouse development can be an effective first step in reengineering or remodeling an organizations legacy systems.

1.13 Check Your Learning
Review Questions

1. The organizational information analysis requirements are met by:

    a. Databases

    b. Data Warehouses

    c. Decision Support Systems

    d. Operating Systems

2. A Warehouse is a structured extensible environment that is periodically updated and maintained for a length of time.

    a. True

    b. False

3. Data Warehousing systems support very sophisticated online analysis including multi-dimensional analysis.

    a. True

    b. False

4. Operational systems are designed for acceptable performance for _____transactions.

    a. On-the-fly

    b. Pre-defined

    c. All

    d. Specific

5. A key attribute of the data within a data warehouse system is that it is loaded on to the warehouse after it has become _____.

    a. Non Volatile

    b. Obsolete

    c. Operational

    d. Redundant

6. Normalization is a warehouse modeling process where the relations or tables are progressively decomposed into smaller relations to a point where all attributes in a relation are very tightly fixed with the primary key of the relation.

    a. True

    b. False

7. The data is logically _____ when it is brought to the data warehouse from the operational systems.

    a. Complete

    b. Incomplete

    c. Transformed

    d. Appended

8. The process of combining data from multiple applications before being moved into a Data Warehouse is referred to as:

    a. Transformation

    b. Combining

    c. Staging

    d. Warehousing

9. The time dimension in the data warehouse serves as a primary cross-referencing attribute.

    a. True

    b. False

10. Data Warehouses are intended to deliver information derived from a variety of operational systems to support the _____ needs of an organization.

    a. Archival

    b. Storage

    c. Business Analysis

    d. None of the Above

EXERCISES

1. What is a Data Warehousing? Explain the organizational need and benefits for deploying data warehousing systems.

2. List down three major driving forces responsible for the widespread growth of data warehousing systems with a brief explanation for each.

3. List down five key attributes of a data warehouse along with a brief explanation.

4. What do you understand by the term "summary views"? List down the advantages of employing summary views.

5. Enumerate on the commonly employed organizational data warehousing tools.

RESEARCH ACTIVITIES

Taking an example of a small organization or an SBU list down the following:

1. Needs and Benefits of implementing warehousing solutions
2. Database Design
3. Interfaces required
4. Access tools required

---

[i] MDC is a non profit consortium of software vendors, developers and end users and provides tactical solution for meta data exchange.

[ii] OMG is an international, open membership, non profit computer industry consortium developing enterprise integration standards for a wide range of technologies. OMG's middleware standards are based on the Common Object Request Broker (CORBA) Architecture and support a wide variety of industries.

In 2000 the two industry organizations jointly announced that MDC will merge with OMG and will discontinue independent operations while merging the two standards

CHAPTER 1 - KNOWLEDGE MAP

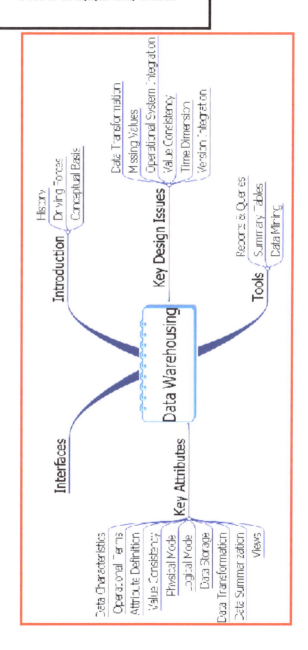

Chapter 2

Data Warehousing Essentials

Data Warehouse Architecture
& Data Modeling

Objectives

This chapter lays the foundation for preparing the blue print for designing a data warehouse. It provides an introduction to the commonly used data analysis techniques and their linkage with the data warehouse architecture. The choice of the technique employed is based on the end user requirements and greatly impacts the modeling of the warehouse. The chapter begins with an introduction to the commonly employed data analysis tools and proceeds to list down the key warehouse components. The various structural options of a data warehouse are also subsequently introduced. Data Warehouse modeling is an important area that requires specific treatise and a model is constructed directly from the Enterprise Data Model, which is the high-level data blueprint describing the organization's integrated information requirements. This ensures that the collective information requirements of the enterprise are represented in the Data Warehouse Model and further each subject area in the Enterprise Data Model has a corresponding Data Warehouse Model component.

The emerging knowledge based economy has spurned organizations to deploy warehousing solutions with the hope of instantly exploiting them to provide tailor made solutions to strategic and operational issues. Thus a small note on multidimensional analysis has been included in this chapter. Multidimensional analysis has become a popular way to extend the capabilities of query and reporting. It provides an alternative to the cumbersome method of submitting multiple *queries and has its data suitably structured to enable fast and easy answers to the questions typically raised.*

The chapter also presents a brief on the Data warehouse Engineering Life Cycle. This would include the enterprise needs identification which is crucial component of the lifecycle. The design & development of operational systems necessitates a clear understanding of the requirements. Of these a lucid perception of the system look, feel and function is very essential. Data Warehouse implementation includes loading the preliminary data, implementing transformation programs, designing an optimal user interface as well as querying and reporting mechanisms and finally supporting the effort by training the end users. Thus this chapter covers the essential knowledge required to design, implement and deploy data warehousing solutions tailor made to suit individual/organizational requirements.

KEY LEARNING'S
☒ Understanding the Data Warehouse Architecture
☒ Data Warehouse Components
☒ Data Modeling Techniques
☒ Data Warehouse Models

Chapter 2

Data Modeling & Analysis

2.1 INTRODUCTION

A data warehouse is designed to provide easy access to high quality data sources. An important thing to note is that a warehouse is not the end objective, but rather the path leading to the end point. The end point is subsequent application of analytical and decision making tools to garner valuable insights from the extracted data. There are several techniques for data analysis that are in commonly employed. These include standard query and reporting and the more advanced multidimensional analysis and data mining techniques and is as illustrated in the figure 2.1 below. These techniques facilitate the formulation and display of query results, multi perspective analysis of data content, pattern discovery while clustering of attributes in the data provides valuable insights to an individual and/or an organization. There are several commonly employed methods of data analysis. The choice of these methods can greatly impact the type of data model selected and it's content. For example for an organization requiring quick information retrieval (Query & Reporting capability) would deploy a model that structures the data in a normalized fashion. Query and reporting capability primarily consists of selecting associated data elements, summarizing them and grouping them by category, and presenting the results using direct table scans. For this type of capability a model with a normalized and/or denormalized data structure would be highly appropriate. Similarly a dimensional data model would be more appropriate if the objective is to perform multidimensional data analysis. This type of analysis requires that the data model support a structure that enables fast and easy access to the data on the basis of any of numerous combinations of analysis dimensions.

Multidimensional analysis requires a data model that facilitates easy access and

KEY POINTS
✓ Data Analysis Methods
✓ Data Warehouse Modeling
✓ Data Analysis Techniques

presents multi dimensional viewing perspectives. The presence of a number of dimensions warrants the need for quick access to the data. If a highly normalized data structure were to be used, many joins would be required between the tables holding the multi dimensional data, thereby significantly degrading system performance. The following example throws further light on this concept. A sales executive needs to know the quantity of a specific product sold on a specific day, in a specific super market, in a specific price range. Then for further analysis he might also need to find the number of super markets selling the specific product, in a specific price range, on the specific day. These two queries require similar information, however one is viewed from a product perspective and the other viewed from the super market perspective. In this case, a dimensional data model would be most appropriate. An understanding of the data and its use will impact the choice of a data model. However in practice it is observed that most organizational implementations employ multiple types of data models to best satisfy the varying requirements of the data warehouse.

2.2 DATA ANALYSIS TECHNIQUES

This section provides an introduction to the commonly used data analysis techniques and their linkage with the data warehouse architecture. The choice of the technique employed is based on the end user requirements and greatly impacts the modeling of the warehouse.

QUERY & REPORTING

The query and reporting tool is one of the **most commonly** employed data analysis technique. Query and reporting analysis is the process of posing a question to be answered, retrieving relevant data from the data warehouse, transforming it into the appropriate context, and displaying it in a readable format. It is primarily driven by analysts who must pose those questions to receive an answer. This process is however considerably different from data mining, which is data driven. Traditionally most queries are two-dimensional or in other words have the capability of handling only two factors simultaneously. The standard sales or marketing queries regarding daily or weekly or monthly product sales figure is an appropriate example of a two-dimensional query. Subsequent queries would then be posed to perhaps determine the quantity of a product was sold by a particular super market chain. The process flow in a standard query and reporting process is aptly illustrated in the following figure 2.2.

Query definition is the process of taking a business question or hypothesis and translating it into a query format that can be used by a particular decision support tool. When the query is executed, the tool generates the appropriate language commands to access and retrieve the requested data, which is returned in a format referred to as an answer set. The data analyst then performs the required calculations and manipulations on the answer set to achieve the desired results. Those results are then formatted to fit into a display or report template that has been selected for ease of understanding by the end user. This template could consist of combinations of text, graphic images, video, and audio. The report is finally delivered to the end user on a desired output media, which could be a hard copy, soft copy or a visual or audio display. The process of query and reporting thus commences with a query definition and ends with a report delivery.

Figure 2.1 - Query & Reporting Process

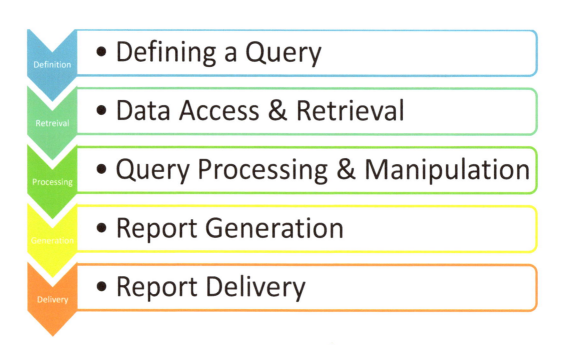

- Definition — • Defining a Query
- Retreival — • Data Access & Retrieval
- Processing — • Query Processing & Manipulation
- Generation — • Report Generation
- Delivery — • Report Delivery

MULTI DIMENSIONAL ANALYSIS

Multidimensional analysis is a method that extends the capabilities of query and reporting tools. This technique employs the use of structured data to enable fast and easy access to answers to typical questions as opposed to submitting multiple queries. For example, the data would be structured to include answers to a question related to the sale of a particular product on a particular day by a particular salesman for a particular super market. Each separate part of that query is referred to as a dimension. The answers to each sub query is pre-computed, within the broad framework, By pre-calculating answers to each subquery within the larger context, multiple answers can be made readily available. The results are not recalculated with each query but are simply accessed and displayed. The result of the query mentioned in the earlier example would automatically answer the following subquery: The quantity of a particular product sold by a particular salesperson.

End users especially those with business orientation find the dimensional data (data categorized by different factors) easier to assimilate and disseminate. Dimensions can have individual entities or a hierarchy of entities, such as region, store, and department. Multidimensional analysis enables users to view a large number of interdependent factors involved in a business problem and to view the data in complex relationships. Typically end users are interested in exploring the data at different levels of detail and this requirement is generally dynamic in nature. The complex relationships are analyzed through an **iterative** process that includes drilling down to lower levels of detail or rolling up to higher levels of summarization and aggregation. The figure 2.3 below demonstrates that the user can start by viewing the total sales for an organization and drill down to view the sales by continent, region, country, and finally by customer. Or, the user could start at customer and roll up through the different levels to finally reach total sales.

Pivoting or changing the dimension of the data can also be employed. Pivoting is

KEY POINT

Pivoting

a data analysis operation whereby a user takes a different viewpoint that is typical of the results of the analysis, changing the way the dimensions are arranged in the result. Like query and reporting, multidimensional analysis continues until no more drilling down or rolling up is performed. The end users have the option of performing drill down or roll up when using multidimensional analysis.

Figure 2.2 - Multi Dimensional Analysis

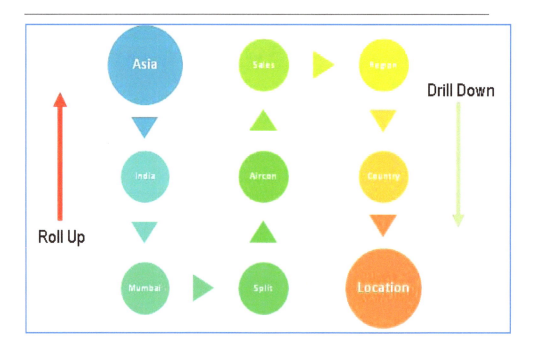

DATA MINING

Data mining is a **data analysis technique**, which is very different from query and reporting well as multidimensional analysis. Using the techniques listed in the above section, a user has to create and execute queries based on hypotheses. Data mining searches for answers to questions that may have not been previously asked. This discovery could take the form of finding significance in relationships between certain data elements. This involves a clustering of specific data elements or other patterns governing the usage of specific sets of data elements. The discovery of these patterns can be followed by the deployment of algorithms to infer rules. These rules can then subsequently be used to generate a model that can predict a desired behavior, identify relationships among the data as well as discover patterns and group clusters of records with similar attributes.

Data mining is employed for **statistical data analysis and knowledge discovery**. The statistical data analysis detects unusual data patterns and applies statistical and mathematical modeling techniques to infer the patterns. The models are then used to forecast and predict. Types of statistical data analysis techniques include:

Knowledge discovery extracts implicit, previously unknown information from the data. This often results in uncovering unknown business facts. Data mining is data driven and unravels a high level of complexity in stored data and data interrelations in the data warehouse that is normally difficult to discover. It offers new insights into the business that may not be discovered with query and reporting or multidimensional analysis and provides users with answers to questions that have never been thought of.

STATISTICAL DATA TECHNIQUES
✓ Linear & Non Linear Analysis
✓ Regression Analysis
✓ Time Series Analysis
✓ Multi Variate Analysis

EXPLORATORY DATA ANALYSIS

Exploratory Data Analysis (EDA) is data analysis approach that employs a variety of techniques predominantly graphical techniques to:

EDA is an approach that is not identical to statistical graphics but lays emphasis on how data analysis should be carried out. The two terms, EDA and statistical analysis are however used almost interchangeably. Statistical graphics is a collection of graphic techniques that focuses on a single

> **E D A**
> - Comprehensively analyze a data set
> - Reveal the underlying structure
> - Extract important variables
> - Identify anomalies
> - Examine underlying assumptions
> - Develop models
> - Determine optimal factor settings

aspect of data characterization. EDA, in comparison, employs a direct approach wherein the data is used to reveal its underlying structure rather than making assumptions of the underlying data model. As opposed to a collection of techniques, EDA presents a methodology that facilitates an analysis of the objects/values to aid identification and interpretation. This is achieved by deploying a compilation of techniques that are graphical in nature with a few quantitative techniques. The need for **graphical interpretation** is fuelled by the desire to facilitate and open ended exploration of the data set including its structural framework while revealing new and often hidden insights into the data. In combination with the natural pattern-recognition capabilities graphics provides a powerful and simple method for data analysis.

2.3 Data Models & Modeling Techniques

In order to analyze the behavior of business processes it is necessary to process a set of numeric values like sales revenue and shipment quantities. There may be also requirements for calculating or scrutinizing quality measures such as customer satisfaction rates, delays in the business processes and delayed or incorrect shipments. There may also be a need for analysis of the effects of business events or transactions with a view of extrapolating predictions for the future. The data displayed may cause the user to formulate another query to clarify the answer or gather more detailed information. This process continues until the desired results are reached. The type of analysis that will be done with the data warehouse can determine the type of model and its contents. Since query, reporting and multidimensional analysis require summarization and **explicit metadata**, it is important that the model contain these elements. Further multidimensional analysis usually entails drilling down and rolling up, so these characteristics need to be present in the model as well. A comprehensible data warehouse model is a precursor to ensuring consistency of results while retaining simplicity of end user tasks. An important point to note is that the deployment of data mining techniques warrants a model that provides for the lowest level of detail.

The graphical representation of the data for an organizational business domain or area of operation is referred to as a data model. The scope

---
N O T E

Key information

---

could include the entire organizational data needs – Enterprise Data Model That area of interest may be as broad as all the integrated data requirements of a complete business organization (**Enterprise Data Model**) or as focused as a single business area (SBU) or application. The data model represents the organizations functional area within the business area (sales in telecom, IT, etc) or a specific domain being analyzed (product delivery, customer satisfaction). The important or recommended characteristics of a good data model are as listed below:

i)   Entities (tables)

ii)   Attributes (columns)

iii)   Data inter-relationships

iv)   Data cardinality, business rules governing data relationships

v)   Entities & attributes definition

vi)   Well defined Primary and Secondary keys

vii)   Graphical

The data model communicates the meaning of the underlying data along with their attributes, inert-relationships and accurate definitions. A data model is the standard and accepted way of analyzing data, designing and implementing databases. The organizational data model does not change drastically over a length of time unless there is a fundamental change in the organization vision/mission. However the data usage and the processes involved can greatly vary across organizations in the same industry. This is despite the fact that their data requirements can be very similar. This similarity of data facilitates the development of template data models that can be adopted by organizations operating in a similar domain. From the above discussion one can infer that the organizational data models are stable while the process models may be volatile. The CASE[12] tools are commonly employed for data modeling. CASE tools

---

[1] Computer-aided software engineering (CASE) tool refers to the holistic software used for automated system software development including design, analysis and programming. The CASE tool provides an automated environment for designing, developing and documenting structured computer programs. It also includes data modelling tools.
2 http://en.wikipedia.org/wiki/Computer-aided_software_engineering

provide the supporting software for development of the model including the graphics, data dictionary, links to other tools and supporting utilities. The function of the data model is to clearly convey data, data relationships, data attributes, and data definitions along with the business rules that governing the data. Data models are the accepted way of representing and designing databases.

TEMPLATE DATA MODELS

Template data models are fully functional pre-designed data models built for a specific industry. These models closely approximate the results achieved from the development of tailor made models for individual organizations. Template data models can be built for every conceivable data-modeling requirement, including the following types of applications:

i)   Enterprise

ii)   Data Warehouse

iii)   Business Area

iv)   DSS/Data Mart

v)   Dimensional

Further the template data models of share the following characteristics:

i)   Constructed for a specific industry or industry segment.

ii)   Clear, unambiguous, detailed and fully attributed.

Template data models are based upon detailed industry analysis that enables fully attributed models to be developed. This attention to detail is what accelerates the planning, analysis and design phase and makes the use of template data models of real value. Each entity should closely approximate a table that a Data Analyst would use to design an application and a Data Base Administrator would use to build that application. Every entity and attribute must be completely defined in conjunction with the organizational requirement and should include appropriate examples. It is not unusual for a suite of industry template data models to be supported by high volumes of documentation. Also adequate care should also be taken to see that every relationship is taken into account and properly named.

NOTE

Key information

Key Features & Advantages

- The typical information technology (IT) project consists of a long planning, analysis, design and implementation phase incorporating a host of hardware, software and staffing activities. The most challenging, expensive and difficult to predict are the planning, analysis and design project phases.

- Research has uncovered that over **60%** of data warehouse implementations failures happen in these initial phases and not as a result of fallacy in the hardware or software selection process. It is in the initial phases that decisions on the data content, its structure and representation with the data warehouse are made.

- There is no method available to shorten the amount of time required for planning, analysis and design. There is no procedure or method to predict the result or the value (ROI) of these initial phases unless a set of detailed, industry-specific template data models are used to bootstrap these activities.

- Template data models provide a close approximation of what would be achieved during that lengthy period at a small fraction of the cost.

- Template data models are the deliverables that is intended to kick-start and dramatically shorten the planning, analysis and design phase.

- The deployment of these models can save the project months of work while effecting massive monetary savings as well.

- Template data models are flexible and are designed to be modified, extended and integrated with other data models.

- The commonly available template data models include the following:

  - Resource estimation
  - Gap analysis
  - Industry Knowledge Transfer
  - Project Planning
  - ROI Estimation
  - Standards Definition
  - Staff Training

- Building data models requires a unique set of skills which includes the following:

  - *Broad industry experience at each level*
  - *Senior data modeling expertise*
  - *Extensive DBA expertise*
  - *System integration exposure*

- The above combination of skills, expertise and long development cycles makes template data models unique. It also makes them extremely valuable in almost all industrial areas including:

1. Banking
2. Financial Services
3. Food & Beverage
4. Insurance
5. Pharmaceutical
6. Products, Goods & Services
7. Retail
8. Semiconductor

Models need to be frequently combined or integrated with other models to satisfy organizational requirements. The data models are developed from a common core of building blocks so they can be rapidly integrated with organizational data structures while providing consistent definitions of customer, distribution channels, geography and other common parameters. The data warehouse, data mart and allied applications must be mapped to the larger organizational context if it is to be successfully integrated with other systems. The larger organizational context is referred to as the '**Enterprise Data Model**'.

ENTERPRISE DATA MODELS[3]

The Enterprise Data Model is primarily employed for strategic planning as well as disseminating the warehouse data requirements throughout the enterprise. It is also used for implementing integrated systems while organizing data in the data warehouse along with the associated structures and applications. The Enterprise Data Model identifies the complete organizational data and is based upon in-depth analysis of business areas, terminology, data relationships, definitions, examples and business rules pertaining to specific industrial domains.

The Enterprise Data Model graphically depicts entities by subject area, keys, attributes, relationships and cardinalities. The Enterprise Data Model should be concise, easy to understand, supported by structured project information as well as definitions and presented graphically. Such a model would provide a point of integration for the entire organization while serving as a powerful tool for understanding the business and planning to make it more efficient and effective. The Enterprise Data Model is **specific to an industrial environment** or domain and provides the integrated primary data requirements of a standard organization operating in the domain. The model contains 4-10 entities representing the business subject area (domain), business functional area, and the key relationships between primary data. A typical Enterprise Data Model would consist of over 400 entities and 2,500 attributes.

BUSINESS AREA MODELS

Business Area Models are detailed data models representing **standard functions** within a specific business domain. The model is developed from a set of core of entities drawn from the higher-level subject area of domain specific Enterprise Data Models. The subject area model is subsequently expanded in scope and detail until its functionality is sufficient to support Decision Support Systems (DSS) or application development related to the functional business area under consideration. The core subject area entities from the Enterprise Data Model form the nucleus upon which detailed Business Area Models are developed. The advantage of developing subject area models directly from the Enterprise Data Model is that it insures that the keys will match and supports the future integration of data with other subject area data models, the Data Warehouse Model or back into the Enterprise Data Model itself. The following are examples of Business Area data models:

- Asset Management
- Bookings & Billings
- Budgeting
- Channel Management
- Commissions Management
- Contract Management
- Customer
- Customer Sales Management
- Financial
- Forecast
- Geography
- HR/Employee
- Inventory
- Manufacturing/Shop Floor Control
- Market
- Marketing Events
- Order
- Pricing
- Problem Reporting
- Product Management
- Prospective Customer Management
- Purchasing
- Training & Education

Business Area Models contain the **greatest level of detail** and represent the low-level details of the data in the hierarchy. The new information is learned about business areas are subsequently added to the corresponding Business Area Model. This information may also be incorporated into the Enterprise Data Model, Data Warehouse Model or application data models. The usage of Business Area Models as a basis for analysis and design provides a solid foundation of industry-specific knowledge that leads to accelerated planning and development. Individual models can easily be combined or integrated to create other models. For example, a "Customer Feedback" prototype data model may be quickly built from individual Business Area Models. Once the Enterprise Data Model and Business Area Model components are in place, it is possible to introduce the Data Warehouse Models. The Data Warehouse Model represents the integrated decision support and information reporting requirements of the business. The Data Warehouse is the center of the decision support and reporting data architecture and represents the ultimate source of clean, consistent data for the entire organization. The Data Warehouse may be surrounded by any number of functional decision support systems or "data marts" serving the associated functional business areas. As data moves from the Data Warehouse to local DSS or "data mart" systems, control of the data is turned over to local administrators. The Data Warehouse remains the consistent source of reliable data.

SUBJECT AREA MODELS

Subject Area Models describe **functional** subject areas that are unique to an organization. Subject Area Models represent the lowest levels of data and provide the design foundation for the data warehouse, data marts, applications development, business analysis and strategic planning. Each Subject Area Model is constructed from a set of core entities drawn from related subject areas in the Enterprise Model. This ensures that Subject Area Models will have common keys, attributes and definitions throughout the enterprise data architecture. This approach also supports integration of existing models and development of new models. The new information learned subsequently is added to the Subject Area Model. It may also be incorporated into the Enterprise Model, Data Warehouse Model or application models. Subject Area Models provides a solid foundation of knowledge for development industry-specific application and information solutions.

2.4 DATA MODELING – KEY STEPS

The Data Warehouse Model represents the actual organization of data within the warehouse. It describes the data structures and their inter-relationships. The domain specific organizational informational requirements are represented by the data model. A domain (business area of an organization) data warehouse model is directly derived from the Enterprise Data Model specific to the operational domain. The Enterprise Data Model logical data structures are the foundation for development of corresponding data warehouse data structures. The Data Warehouse data structures model the organizational data structure. Following is a list of characteristics of a data warehouse model:

- Stable data over a length of time
- Summarized data for DSS, clean and reliable data for data marts
- Integrated data from multiple sources

- Design driven by evolving information needs
- Business area, function or subject orientation
- Integrated organizational information access
- Granularity of data suitable for analysis over extended periods of time
- Multiple levels of summarization
- Iterative construction grouped by subject area

The Data Warehouse is the ultimate source of clean, consistent data for the entire organization. It forms the backbone of the DSS and allied analysis systems. The Data Warehouse may be surrounded by any number of functional DSS or "data marts" serving the associated functional business area. As data moves from the Data Warehouse to local DSS or "**data mart**" systems, control of the data is turned over to local administrators. The Data Warehouse remains a consistent source of data over time for the business organization and is independent of the local data processing. Data warehouse deign commences with the analysis of the organizational core business areas that would be the major contributory data source to the warehouse. Business Area data Models describe lower levels of detailed data appropriate to building applications and DSS/Data Marts for a explicit business domains. These models are constructed from a set of core of entities derived from subject areas in the Enterprise Data Model. This ensures that Business Area Models will be based on common key entities, have common keys, attributes and definitions through the data architecture. This approach also supports consistent integration of existing data models and development of new data models. Each subject area in the Enterprise Data Model has a corresponding Data Warehouse Model component.   A Data Warehouse Model can be implemented in two distinct functional levels:

i)   Decision Support Data

ii)   Summarized Data

The Level 1 DSS data model describes data at the lowest level of detail appropriate for detailed analysis and decision-making as illustrated in the following examples:

---

o   Orders from a specific Customer for a period of time"

o   "Quantity sales for a specific Channel for a period of time"

o   "Sales revenue from the sales of a specific Product via a Channel during a period"

The Summary model depicts **summarized** data defined in the DSS model. The top management of an enterprise generally employs the summary data generated for strategic decision making. Some of the questions posed at this level include the following:

---

o   Total Revenues- sales across all products and customers for a specific period "

o   "Total Orders across all accounts for a specific period "

o   "Total Sales Quantity across all distribution channels for a specific period "

o   "Sales Revenues for a specific product over a specific period "

The listing down of the key organizational decision making factors is the

precursor to building a template for the Data Warehouse Model. These factors may include following:

- o Customer Segments
- o Markets and Market Segments
- o Geography Definition
- o Product Families
- o Product Lines Definition

The following figures 2.3 illustrate the key steps in constructing a data warehouse:

Figure 2.3 – Building a Data Warehouse

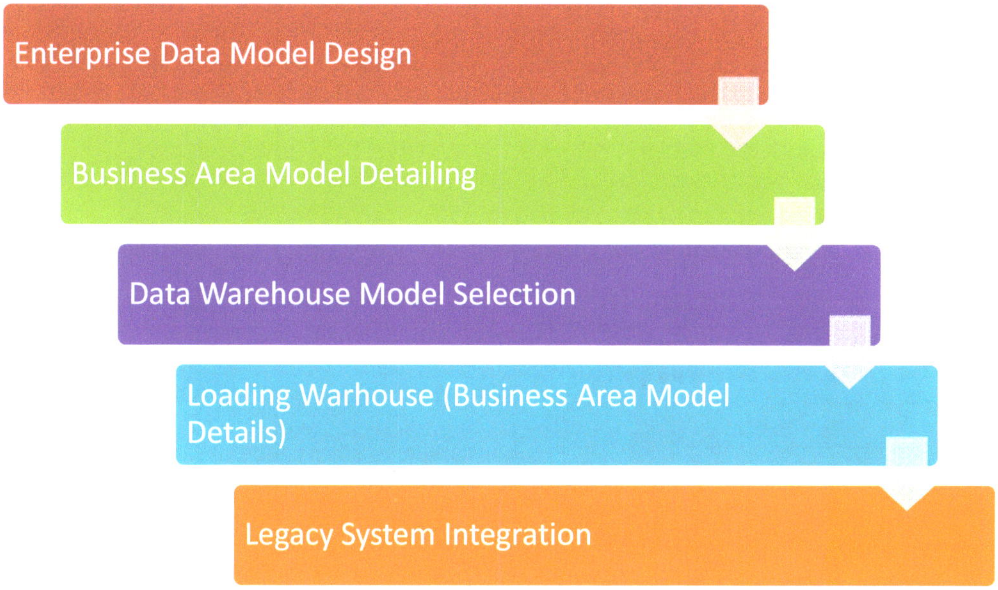

Enterprise Data Model Design

Business Area Model Detailing

Data Warehouse Model Selection

Loading Warhouse (Business Area Model Details)

Legacy System Integration

The Data Warehouse is built from existing template data model components representing the way the business intends to do business, which are then modified to meet the realities of legacy data and existing applications. The process is greatly accelerated by utilizes standard industry data building blocks that can readily be modified, extended or integrated to meet specific data requirements. Each of these models can be modified and contributes data to related models. The models are broken up into functional building blocks thereby facilitates parallel processing in multiple areas. Product data can be designed without waiting for the final Customer data structures. The foreign key relationships are defined immediately while the channel values can be defined later. The level of detail in the Business Area Models is consistent with that of the DSS/data marts. This makes it relatively easy to develop DSS/data marts that dovetail with the Data Warehouse. It also makes it simple to promote data structures from the Business Area Models into the Data Warehouse Model or related Business Area Models.

2.5   DATA WAREHOUSE – STRUCTURE & COMPOSITION

A data warehouse forms the primary repository of an organization's historical data or acts as the corporate memory of the organization. A data warehouse is optimized for being integrated with Online Analytical Processing (OLAP) systems. The warehouse contains the data which is used by the OLAP systems or the enterprise Decision Support Systems (DSS). The data warehouse contains the raw material for the organizational DSS. The data warehouse is

DATA WAREHOUSE – KEY CHARACTERISTICS
✓   Subject Oriented
✓   Time Variant
✓   Non Volatile
✓   Integrated

optimized for reporting and analysis (OLAP) in comparison to operational systems that are optimized for simplicity and speed of modification (Online Transaction Processing or OLTP). This is achieved through the heavily normalized databases and an entity-relationship model. The data in Data Warehouses are heavily denormalized, summarized and/or stored in a dimension-based model in order to achieve acceptable query response times. Following are some of the important characteristics of a data warehouse:

1. **Subject-Oriented**

   The data in the database is organized so that all the data elements relating to the same real-world event or object are linked together

2. **Time-variant**

   The changes to the data in the database are tracked and recorded so that reports can be produced showing changes over time

3. **Non-volatile**

   The data in the database is never over-written or deleted, but retained for future reporting

4. **Integrated**

   The database contains consistent data from most or all of an organization's operational applications.

2.5.1 DATA WAREHOUSE STRUCTURE

We will initially have a look at the structure of a data warehouse before proceeding to understand its key components. A data warehouse consists of two major parts as outlined below:

PHYSICAL STORE

The physical store is a server based database that is employed for querying and includes an OLAP database for running reports. The physical store for the Data Warehouse includes one database that is employed for running the SQL queries. The physical store contains all the data that has been imported from different sources.

LOGICAL SCHEMA

The logical schema is the **conceptual model** that maps onto the data in the physical store. The logical schema provides an understandable view of the data in the data warehouse, and supports an efficient import process. For example, a developer can use the logical schema to modify the location of data stored in the underlying physical tables. A developer interacts with the logical schema in order to add, update, or delete data in the data warehouse. The end user need not be aware of the logical schema. A logical schema includes the following:

Class

Class refers to a **logical collection** of data members.

For example, the **Administrator_User** class contains data members with administrative system privileges.

Data member

The data member is a structure that stores a piece of data. For example, the **Employee_Number** of the data member of the **Administrator_User** class stores the contact numbers for users with administrative system privileges.

Relation

A relation is a **connection** between two classes depicting a parent-child relationship. This relationship defines the number of instances of each class, and it provides the mechanism for sharing data members between classes. For example, **Administrator_User** is a parent to the child class Request. There can be many requests for one authorized user.

The logical schema uses classes, data members, relations, and other data structures to map data in the physical store. The interrelationship between the two entities is illustrated in the following figure 2.4below:

Figure 2.4 - Data Warehouse – Logical Schema

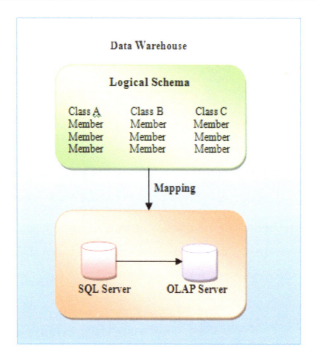

2.5.2   DATA WAREHOUSE KEY COMPONENTS

The primary components of a data warehouse are illustrated in the figure and described in more detail in the following section:

1. Data Sources

A data source refers to any electronic repository of information that contains relevant organizational data. This would include systems employed for OLTP as well as storage of operational data like main frames, mini frames, relational data base systems (Oracle, Microsoft SQL, IBM DB2), PC based databases like Microsoft Access, Microsoft Excel and any other electronic store of data. Data needs to be passed from these systems to the data warehouse either on a transaction-by-transaction basis for real-time data warehouses or on a regular cycle (e.g. daily or weekly) for offline data warehouses. Further organizational data embodied in physical documents would need to be digitized before porting onto the warehouse.

DATA WAREHOUSE - KEY COMPONENTS

- ✓ Data Sources
- ✓ Data Transformation Layer
- ✓ Storage
- ✓ Analysis Tools
- ✓ Metadata
- ✓ Operational Processes
- ✓ Optional Components

2. Data Transformation Layer

The data transformation layer is the subsystem responsible for the extraction of data from the data sources (source systems), transformation from the source format and structure into the target (data warehouse) format and structure and subsequently loading the transformed data into the data warehouse. Alternately another technique that is widely employed is to relegate the transformation of the source format and structure to the last stage of the transformation layer. Under this approach, the data is first extracted from the sources, loaded into the target data warehouse and then transformed into the final format and structure. This process is popularly referred as **ELT** (Extract, Load and Transform).

3. **Storage**

The data warehouse is a normally structured relational database that must be organized to hold information in a structure that best supports not only query and reporting, but also advanced analysis techniques, like data mining. Most data warehouses hold information for at least a year and some may also be used for highly extended periods, depending on the business/operations data retention requirement. As a result a very large storage capacity may be required for the data warehouses. The retail and the telecommunications industries generally own very large data warehoused in the **Terabytes** (TB) range. The primary determinant of the size and shape of the data warehouse is the size and shape of the business problem. The size and shape of the data warehouse in a given enterprise is a function of the experience and maturity of the industry as to the use of business intelligence for decision support and competitive advantage as well as the length of storage.

4. **Analysis Tools**

The data in the data warehouse must be disseminated within the organizational employees for it to be useful. This information/knowledge dissemination can be performed by a very large number of software applications or can be tailor made to suit organizational needs. These applications include:

a. **Business Intelligence Tools**

These are software applications that simplify the process of development and production of business reports based on data warehouse data.

b. **Executive Information Systems**

These are software applications that are used to display complex business metrics and information in a graphical way to allow rapid understanding.

c. **OLAP Tools**

OLAP tools form data into logical multi-dimensional structures and allow users to select which dimensions to view data.

d. **Analytical Applications**

These are generally industry or domain specific applications that combine simple to complex ad-hoc reporting as well as simulation capabilities.

e. **Data Mining**

Data mining tools are software that allows users to perform detailed mathematical and statistical calculations on detailed data warehouse data to detect trends, identify patterns and analyze data.

5. **Metadata**

Metadata or **"data about data"** is used to provide pointers regarding that status and the information contained within a warehouse to its operators and users. It is also used as a means of integrating incoming data to the warehouse and further as a tool to update and refine the underlying warehouse model. Examples of data warehouse metadata include table and column names, their detailed descriptions, their connection to business meaningful names, the most recent data load date, the business meaning of a data item and the number of users that are logged in currently.

6. **Operational Processes**

Operational processes comprise of the tasks of loading, manipulating and extracting data from the data warehouse. It also covers user management, security, capacity management and related functions

7. Optional Components

In addition to the above mentioned primary data warehouse components the following components may be present in some data warehouses:

a. Data Marts

A data mart is a **physical database** (either on the same hardware as the data warehouse or on a separate hardware platform) that receives all its information from the data warehouse. The purpose of a Data Mart is to provide a sub-set of the data warehouse's data for a specific purpose or to a specific sub-group of the organization. A data mart is technically exactly like a data warehouse but it serves a different business purpose: it either holds information for only part of a company (such as a division), or it holds a small selection of information for the entire company (to support extra analysis without slowing down the main system).

b. Logical Data Marts

A logical data mart is a filtered view of the main data warehouse but does not physically exist as a separate data copy. This approach to data marts delivers the same benefits as a physical data mart but has the additional advantage of not requiring additional disk space. Further it is always as current with data as the main data warehouse. However the primary disadvantage with this approach is that Logical Data Marts can have **slower response times** than physical ones.

c. **Operational Data Store**

An Operational Data Store (ODS) is an integrated database of operational data. Its sources include legacy systems, and it contains current or near-term data. An ODS may contain 30 to 60 days of information, while a data warehouse typically contains years of data. They are employed in some data warehouse architectures to provide near-real-time reporting capability in the event that the Data Warehouse's loading time or architecture prevents it from being able to provide near-real-time reporting capability.

2.6 DATA WAREHOUSE ARCHITECTURE

A Data Warehouse Architecture (**DWA**) is a method of representing the overall structure of data, including the communication framework, processing mechanism and presentation format that exists for end-user computing within an enterprise. The architecture is made up of a number of interconnected parts that includes the following:

DATA WAREHOUSE
ARCHITECTURE

---

1. Operational Database   External Database Layer
2. Information Access Layer
3. Data Access Layer
4. Data Directory (Metadata) Layer
5. Process Management Layer
6. Application Messaging Layer
7. Data Warehouse Layer
8. Data Staging Layer
9. Data Sources

Figure 2.5 Data Warehouse Architecture

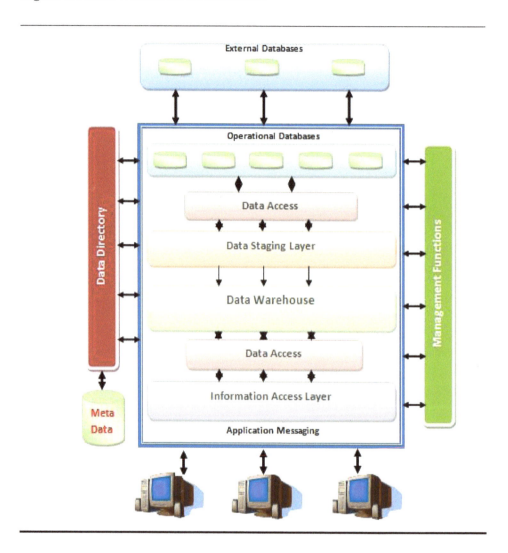

1. OPERATIONAL DATABASE / EXTERNAL DATABASE LAYER

Operational systems are employed to process data while supporting critical operational needs. The operational databases are historically created to provide an efficient processing structure for a relatively small number of well-defined business transactions. The limited focus of operational systems makes it difficult for other management applications to interact with the operational databases. This difficulty in accessing the operational data is amplified by the fact that many operational systems are often 10 to 15 years old and the systems employed to access this data would itself have become obsolete. The goal of data warehousing is to free the information that is locked up in the operational databases and combine it with information from other, often external, sources of data. Increasingly, large organizations are acquiring additional data from outside databases. This information may include demographic, econometric, competitive and purchasing trends.

2. INFORMATION ACCESS LAYER

The Information Access layer of the Data Warehouse Architecture is the interface with the end user. More specifically this layer represents the tools that the end-user normally uses day to day, e.g., Excel, Lotus Suite, Microsoft Access, SAS, etc. This layer also includes the **hardware and software** involved in displaying and printing reports, spreadsheets, graphs and charts for analysis and presentation. The last few years have witnessed tremendous growth in the information access layer with the end users having access to powerful computing devices. Further sophisticated tools facilitate enhanced analysis and presentation of data. There however exists the complex issue of making the raw data contained in operational systems available easily and seamlessly to end-user tools. A work around to this problem is to deploy a common data language throughout the enterprise.

3. DATA ACCESS LAYER

The data access layer is primarily involved with facilitating the interface between the information access layer and the operational layer. The commonly employed data language is SQL, originally developed by IBM as a query language, which has become the de facto standard for data interchange. One of the key developments in the last few years has been the emergence of a series of data access filters like EDA/SQL that make it possible to access nearly all DBMS's and data file systems, relational or non-relational using SQL. These filters make it possible for the modern day information access tools to access the database management systems that contain historic data. The data access layer is vendor as well as protocol independent and spans different DBMS and file systems on the same hardware. One of the successful data warehousing strategy is to provide end-users with "**universal data access**" wherein access any or all of the necessary data (subject to access privileges) is possible regardless of location or tools employed. This Layer is also responsible for interfacing access tools with operational databases.

4. DATA DIRECTORY (METADATA) LAYER

In order to provide for universal data access, it is absolutely necessary to maintain some form of data directory or repository of meta-data information. Meta-data is the **data about data** within the enterprise. In order to have a fully functional warehouse, it is necessary to have a variety of meta-data available. This would include data about the end-user views of data and data about the operational databases. The end-users would be able to access data from the data warehouse or any of the organizational operational databases transparently without having to know where that data resides or the form in which it is stored.

5. PROCESS MANAGEMENT LAYER

The Process Management Layer is involved with **scheduling** the various tasks to be accomplished in building and maintaining the data warehouse and the associated data directory information. The Process Management Layer can be thought of as the scheduler or the high-level job controller for multiple processes/procedures required for keeping the contents of the data warehouse updated.

6. APPLICATION MESSAGING LAYER

The Application Message Layer, functioning as a **middleware** in the warehousing system, is responsible for information exchange within the enterprise computing network. This layer contains the networking protocols and can also be used to isolate operational as well as informational applications from the data formats on either end. Application Messaging can, which is the underlying transport system, can also be used to collect transactions or messages and deliver them to a certain location at a certain time.

7. DATA WAREHOUSE (PHYSICAL) LAYER

The data warehouse represents the **logical or virtual** view of the underlying data. In many cases the data warehouse would not be storing the data which may be physically on a different platform altogether. The core of the warehouse is where the actual data used primarily for informational uses resides. In a Physical Data Warehouse, copies, in some cases multiple copies, of operational and or external data are actually stored in a form that is easy to access and is highly flexible. In earlier days the data warehouses were stored on main frames. However in the current scenario they may be located on client/server platforms or in some case separate networks referred to as **storage area networks** (SAN).

8. DATA STAGING LAYER

The **final component** of the Data Warehouse Architecture is **Data Staging**. Data Staging is also referred to as copy management or replication management. It includes all of the processes necessary to **select, edit, summarize, combine and load** a data warehouse with information or access data from operational and/or external databases. Data staging normally involves the scripting of complex access routines or programs. However the emergence of data warehousing tools has simplified this process. Data Staging may also involve data quality analysis programs and filters that identify patterns and data structures within existing operational data.

Every single data element in the physical design model is associated with a logical counterpart in the logical strategic information model. A critical part of designing the Data Warehouse architecture is reverse engineering the existing operational systems of record to match the physical design models in the architecture repository. This provides the basis for gap analysis and defining transformation requirements.

2.7 DATA WAREHOUSE ENGINEERING – LIFE CYCLE

NOTE

Key information

The data warehousing lifecycle consists of **five major phases,** illustrated in the figure below that includes: **Design, Prototype, Deploy, Operationalize and Modify**. The life cycle commences with the design stage that includes the analysis of the existing enterprise data, evaluation of template data models, end user interviews to elicit operational requirements, identification of metrics related to the business, user and expected system performance and culminates with the design of the physical and logical schema. In the prototype development stage a

1. ENTERPRISE NEEDS IDENTIFICATION
2. DETERMINING MEASUREMENT CYCLES
3. MEASURES VALIDATION
4. DATA CONFLICTS RESOLUTION
5. METADATA DEFINITION
6. DATA SOURCE IDENTIFICATION
7. TECHNOLOGY FRAMEWORK
8. INTEGRATION & TRANSFORMATION PROGRAMS
9. WAREHOUSE SECURITY
10. USER INTERFACES

group comprising of members at all tiers of the organizational hierarchy including strategic decision makers, administrators and end users is formulated and their inputs crystallized to develop a working model of the warehouse or a data mart.

This model is further used for gap analysis. After the approval from the target group the prototype is scaled up to an enterprise level or deployed at SBU level based on organizational requirements. This step is complemented by the development of extensive documentation, training, system integration, system optimization and allied activities. Stage 4 related to the routing maintenance of the warehouse along with the related activities of performance tuning and optimization as well as backup schedules. The final stage of the life cycle relates to the upgradation or changes to the warehouse architecture in response to changing business or technology landscape. This stage is continual in nature. The key activities in the engineering of a warehouse, and illustrated in the following figure 2.6 are as detailed below:

Figure 2.6   Data Warehousing Life Cycle

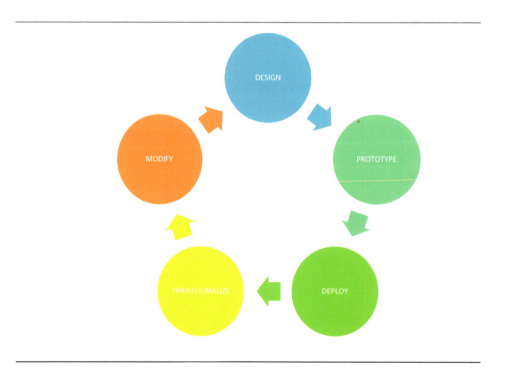

1. ENTERPRISE NEEDS IDENTIFICATION

An important constituent of the engineering life cycle for a data warehouse is the enterprise need identification. The design of a data warehouse requires inputs from multiple individuals as well as user and management groups as opposed to routine operational systems with only single user group involvement. This can lead to the emergence of multiple and often **divergent views** or inputs related to the data warehouse design. This calls for the precise or accurate identification of the enterprise needs which is critical to the success of the data warehousing system.

An organizations strategic business plan would form the basis for the warehouse strategic information needs assessment. This information can be gathered through interviews with key enterprise managers and analysis of other pertinent documentation available. The commencement of the warehousing project should be followed by a series of facilitated focus group sessions to refine or modify the preliminary enterprise information that was elicited from business plans and executive interviews. These discussions would involve the corporate decision-makers who would be among the primary targeted end user groups.

2. DETERMINING MEASUREMENT CYCLES

The enterprise warehouse definition measures include the definition of time cycles or periods for the assessment, processing as well as the storage of enterprise warehouse data. Depending upon the operational domain of the organization under consideration this could be daily, weekly, fortnightly, monthly, quarterly, yearly or any other intermediate period. This time definition would vary between organizations. For example the Government of India (GOI) - Ministry of Economic Affairs in determining the economic trends would employ monthly, quarterly and annual timelines. In contrast the Ministry of Health and Family Affairs would require access to historical data, which may range from couple of years to decades, to formulate meaningful statistics for examination of the population explosion. A telephony service provider may employ hourly measures and may retain only few weeks of information on operational systems.

3. MEASURES VALIDATION

Once the enterprise needs identification is complete it is a good practice to ensure their communication throughout the enterprise. This ensures that the enterprise needs including the process definitions and the critical success factors are made transparent throughout the organization. Thus all the organizational knowledge workers are precisely aware of the metrics governing the success of the warehousing projects along with its measurement parameters. This process would also be beneficial to the organizational knowledge workers who would not be directly involved in the warehousing project but would be involved in the backend processing or providing the raw data for the warehouse. These individuals would also be able to provide valuable feedbacks that could be used to refine the measures further.

4. DATA CONFLICTS RESOLUTION

There exists a possibility for organizational data conflicts that may exist due to **ambiguity** in the usage of key terminologies. Most of the organizations do not have a well defined nomenclature to be followed by all the departments and SBU's. To illustrate this point let us take the example of a service organization – The term 'customer' may imply an organization for the sales department, an organization or an individual who is being billed for the accounting department, an individual for the product development team. A well defined Data Warehouse model, cannot allow data definition conflicts that may arise due to the usage of **homonyms, synonyms or any other naming terminologies**, throughout the organization. Thus in the above example there cannot be an enterprise level definition for the term 'customer'. It is therefore imperative to provide a clear and unambiguous definition for every warehouse data entity along with a description of its usage, methods of derivation, categorization and timelines. These activities are critical to building a clear understanding of an enterprise's measures. The resulting enterprise architecture model, which links the enterprise needs with the warehouse data entities and enterprise rules, can be used as the basis for documentation and information dissemination to the to the enterprise users.

5. METADATA DEFINITION

The data warehouse architecture design commences after the definition and the subsequent documentation of the enterprise needs measures and critical success factors. This activity necessitates the active involvement of the user groups through facilitated design sessions. The process initiates with the definition of the warehouse metadata. In lay man terms metadata can be defined as 'Information about the data' in the warehouse. The important characteristics of the warehouse metadata are that they should be **contextual** (related to time), **accurate**, **highly reliable**, **versioned** (ability to archive data) and also include metadata about the **quality** of the warehouse data. The two primary types of Data Warehouse metadata are as outlined below:

i)   Structural Metadata

Enterprise measures provide an **insight** to the data entities to be included within the warehouse. It also helps in identifying the data entities that need to be aggregated. The number and the types of data aggregation categories in a warehouse will depend directly upon the organizational requirements. This is explained with the help of an example in the paragraph below. Structural data is used to create and maintain the data warehouse.

Structural Metadata is used to represent the **structural framework** of a complex object. This representation could be physical and/or logical. A good example would be the organization of the contents of this book into chapters. The boundaries over the coverage of the chapters are fixed along with the relationship with the other chapters. The structural metadata completely describes the structure of the warehouse along with the associated content. The starting point for the building of structural metadata is the listing of data entities along with their characteristics and inter-relationships.

The type of individuals that provide inputs to the warehouse design also plays an important role in the final outcome of the warehouse structure and specifically on the number of aggregation categories. Individuals representing the top management represent "*Strategic thinking*" and are interested in higher level abstractions of data. These individuals require answers to broad level questions or the 'abstract view and hence require only a very few aggregation categories. The procedures to 'roll-up' or abstract or aggregate data based on strategic inputs can however be complex. In sharp contrast individuals representing the 'line function' or the operational workforce of an organization require access to every measure grouped by category that employed in their domain. These individuals therefore require access to a fairly large numbers of aggregation categories. However the complexity of these categories would be less.

The system of record for the data entities within the data warehouse are identified by the structural metadata. In addition the logic for integration and transformation logic for moving an entity from its system of record to the data warehouse is also described. Further the schedule for refreshing or updating each of the data entities along with their archive requirements are also specified by the structural data. From this discussion it is fairly evident that a change in the data entity would result in a corresponding change in the structural metadata. However, as listed at the beginning of this section, it is important or even mandatory to retain the information regarding the changes and provide appropriate access to them as required. This is required to ensure that the structural metadata is contextual.

In addition to the information listed above, the structural metadata would also include performance metrics for applications and queries. These metrics are employed by developers for time estimation (length of time to execute a query or run a warehousing application) as well as performance optimization of the data warehouse. These metrics are also used for performance optimization of a Data Warehouse.

ii)   **Access Metadata**[3]

The **dynamic linkage** between a data warehouse and the end user applications, which interact with it, is provided by the access metadata. The enterprise nomenclature (standard terms, user defined terms and aliases) along with the enterprise measures are represented by the access metadata. The information regarding the location of the warehouse servers along with their description, databases, detailed data as well as the summaries are included within the access metadata. In addition the rule for navigating the enterprise dimension views (drilling up/down) along with the subject hierarchies (e.g. product, channels or customers) are also provided by the access metadata while also supporting custom user defined queries and/or computations. The access metadata also includes access restrictions governing the display, modifications, analysis or distribution of standard as well as custom queries, computations or summaries.

---

[3] A. Perkins, Developing a Data Warehouse, the Enterprise Engineering Approach, Visible Systems Corporation, 1995-96

6. DATA SOURCE IDENTIFICATION

The enterprise data warehouse architecture also defines or identifies the source of **raw data** that would be moved into the warehouse while also ensuring the consistency of the data entities and the transformation routines. This identification of the data sources (systems of record) of the warehouse data serves as a validation point for the enterprise measures.

7. TECHNOLOGY FRAMEWORK

A robust technology framework is a precursor to a stable organizational warehousing platform. The technology framework includes both the hardware as well as the software architecture. The hardware architecture includes the server environment, their placement, dedicated communication lines, backup mechanisms, storage devices and configurations (RAID, SAN...), authentication framework (centralized setup versus distributed, usage of authentication servers like RADIUS) as well as the backup power supplies. The software architecture would dictate the choice of the operating system environment, application software including the analytical software (Client/Server environment) and multi dimensional access technologies. .It would also include the applications or programs required to move the data into the warehouse, transformation routines and access control mechanisms along with the user interfaces and applications. Some of the key considerations for determining a suitable hardware platform the warehouse include the following:

- The size of the warehouse

- Platforms to be supported and scalability issues
- System optimization and performance
- Application support

8. INTEGRATION & TRANSFORMATION PROGRAMS

The raw operational data cannot be directly loaded onto a warehouse. These application specific data must be converted to enterprise specific data before they can be used by end users of the warehouse. This is performed by the integration and transformation routines. The data from the sources identified have to be initially populated onto the data warehouse. Subsequently the contents of the warehouse need to be frequently updated. This process is achieved through the usage of integration and transformation programs that pull out data from the organizational operational as well as archival databases and systems. A single program can be employed for the initial population of the data warehouse as well as the periodic updation. However there may be certain cases that may warrant the use of separate programs. This is especially true in cases where the warehouse initial load, from operational systems, is very extensive and may severely degrade the performance of the existing users logged in. Also in case the warehouse updates are not too frequent and not significantly large it may be good option to use separate programs. Further the loading of warehouse data from archival systems as well as historical data from operational data systems is usually a non recurring activity and is done using separate programs/routines. The standard industrial practice is to use a set of programs for initially populating the warehouse and another set of programs to ensure its periodic updation. As is obvious, the programs for updating the warehouse are simpler than the load programs, and hence consume lesser system resources. In many cases the updation routines may be actually built onto operational systems to ensure the automatic updation of changes in a real time fashion. Many organizations opt for in-house development of the integration/transformation routines to ensure tighter integration with their operational systems. This option also helps organizations develop extensive documentation which may be helpful in case reconfigurations are required at a later date. In contrast the off-the-shelf programs may not be fully documented, be difficult to integrate with enterprise systems and difficult if not impossible to reconfigure.

9. WAREHOUSE SECURITY

In contrast to organizational databases the enterprise data warehouse is read-only. This implies that developers need not be concerned with the management of creation, updating and deletion capabilities. There however exists a need address the trade off between protecting the organizational intangible assets against unauthorized access while fostering effective organizational information dissemination to ensure effective utilization of knowledge resources. One of the solutions is to have an access controlled environment with different levels of users accorded a differing set of privileges based on need. For example access to the base data of the warehouse may be restricted to only administrators and/or developers while the other users would have access to derivations and summaries. In addition to access security, an enterprise must be concerned with physical security for its Data Warehouse. Because its contents are an extremely valuable organizational intangible resource, they must be protected against loss and damage. This protection is available in many forms ranging from simple backup and off-site storage strategies to installation of uninterrupted power supplies to the deployment redundant array of disks (RAID) for storage.

10. USER INTERFACES

The data from the warehouse is accessed by users to generate useful information through well designed user interfaces. These user interfaces plays an important role altering the perception of the end users about the data warehouse. The guiding criteria for developing an effective user interface is its simplicity or are ease of use and performance. The deployment of graphical user interfaces (GUI) facilitates the development of a menus based hierarchical interfaces that is simple to use. In order to ensure enhanced performance developers must ensure that the hardware/software platform fully supports and is optimized for every chosen user interface. One of the prime selection criteria for user interfaces is the analysis of the information needs and the level of computer literacy of potential users. A good 'rule of thumb' is to employ simple and highly graphic interfaces for users who require access to highly summarized data while providing detailed data users a more complex but less graphical tools. The final requirements would be supports to the warehouse access metadata. An optimal user interface facilitates fast information retrieval in the desired format.

2.8 Recommended Reading

Books

1. Hoberman Steve, Data Modeling Made Simple: 2nd Edition Technics Publications, ISBN-13: 978-0977140060
2. Carlis Vincent John, Maguire Joseph and Carlis John, Mastering Data Modeling, Addison-Wesley Publishing Company, ISBN: 020170045X
3. Hirschheim Rudy, Klein K Heinz and Lyytien Kalle, Information Systems Development and Data Modeling – Conceptual and Philosophical Foundations, Cambridge University Press, 2008, ISBN-13: 978 – 0521063353
4. Reingruber Michael, Reingruber and Gary Gregory, The Data Modeling Handbook: A Best-Practice Approach to Building Quality Data Models Book Description, John Wiley & Sons, 1994, ISBN-13:978-0471052906
5. Simpson Graeme and Witt Graham, Data Modeling Essentials, 3rd Edition, Morgan Kaufmann, 2004, ISBN-13: 978-0126445510

URL

http://www.agiledata.org/essays/dataModeling101.html

http://www.1keydata.com/datawarehousing/toolreporting.html

http://www.inderscience.com

http://www.oracle.com/technology/books/pdfs/powell_dwtuning_ch01.pdf

http://en.wikipedia.org/wiki/Data_modeling

http://en.wikipedia.org/wiki/Data_analysis

http://www.agiledata.org/essays/agileDataModeling.html

http://www.amazon.com/exec/obidos/ASIN/0932633293/ambysoftinc

http://www.amazon.com/exec/obidos/ASIN/0387229507/ambysoftinc/

2.9 Referred Standards

Industry Standard Data Models (ISDM)

Method for an Integrated Knowledge Environment (MIKE 2.0)[4i]

2.10 Key Terms [Nomenclature]

Access Metadata

Application Messaging Layer

Business Area Models

CASE

Class

Data Access Layer

Data Directory Layer

Data Marts

Data Mining

Data Staging

Data Transformation Layer

Data Warehouse Architecture (DWA)

Data Warehouse Layer

Decision Support Systems (DSS)

---

[4] Source URL <http://mike2.openemthodology.org/wiki/What_is_MIKE2.0>

EDA/SQL

Enterprise Data Model

Explicit Metadata

Exploratory Data Analysis (EDA)

Extract, Load and Transform (ELT)

Homonyms

Information Access Layer

Information Technology (IT)

International Business Machines (IBM)

Knowledge Discovery

Logical Data Marts

Logical schema

Metadata

Multidimensional Analysis

Online Analytical Processing (OLAP)

Online Transaction Processing (OLTP)

Operational Data Store (ODS)

Operational Database

Physical store

Pivoting

Process Management Layer

Query & Reporting

RADIUS

RAID

Storage Area Networks (SAN)

Small Business Unit (SBU)

Statistical Data Analysis

Subject Area Models

Summary Model

Synonyms

Terabytes (TB)

2.11 SUMMARY

This chapter laid the foundation for preparing the blue print for designing a data warehouse. It provides an introduction to the commonly used data analysis techniques and their linkage with the data warehouse architecture. The key learning's from this chapter are as listed:

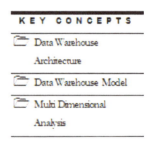

KEY CONCEPTS

- Data Warehouse Architecture
- Data Warehouse Model
- Multi Dimensional Analysis

- A data warehouse is designed to provide easy access to high quality data sources. An important thing to note is that a warehouse is not the end objective, but rather the path leading to the end point. The end point is subsequent application of analytical and decision making tools to garner valuable insights from the extracted data.

- Multidimensional analysis is employed to extend the capabilities of query and reporting tools. This technique employs the use of structured data to enable fast and easy access to answers to typical questions as opposed to submitting multiple queries.

- An organizational data model does not change drastically over a length of time unless there is a fundamental change in the organization vision/mission. The data usage and the processes involved can however vary greatly across enterprises within the same industrial domain, despite having commonality in their data requirements. This similarity of data facilitates the development of template data models that can be adopted by organizations operating in a similar domain.

- A Data Warehouse Model represents the actual organization of data within the warehouse. It describes the data structures and their inter-relationships. The domain specific organizational informational requirements are represented by the data model.

- A data warehouse forms the primary repository of an organization's historical data or acts as the corporate memory of the organization. A data warehouse is optimized for being integrated with transaction processing systems.

- The Data Warehouse Architecture represents the overall structure of data, including the communication framework, processing mechanism and presentation format that exists for end-user computing within an enterprise.

2.12 Check Your Learning
Review Questions

1. A data warehouse is designed to provide easy access to high quality data sources:

    a. False

    b. True

2. An organization requiring quick information retrieval (Query & Reporting capability) would deploy a model that structures the data in a:

    a. Normalized Form

    b. De-Normalized Form

3. A _____ would be more appropriate if the objective is to perform multidimensional data analysis.

    a. Enterprise Data Model

    b. Subject Data Model

    c. Dimensional Data Model

    d. Logical Data Model

4. The most commonly employed data analysis technique is:

    a. Query & Reporting

    b. Data Mining

    c. Multi Dimensional Analysis

    d. KDD

5. Data mining is a data analysis technique, which is very different from query and reporting well as multidimensional analysis :
    a. True
    b. False

6. The different types of statistical data analysis techniques include:
    a. Linear and nonlinear analysis
    b. Regression analysis
    c. Multivariate analysis
    d. _____

7. The _____ are fully functional pre-designed data models built for a specific industry
    a. Enterprise Data Models
    b. Template Data Models
    c. Subject Data Models
    d. Physical Data Models

8. The _____ is primarily employed for strategic planning as well as disseminating the warehouse data requirements throughout the enterprise.
    a. Enterprise Data Model
    b. Template Data Model
    c. Subject Data Model
    d. Physical Data Model

9. The _____are detailed data models representing standard functions within a specific business domain.
   a. Enterprise Data Models
   b. Template Data Models
   c. Subject Data Models
   d. Business Data Models

10. The _____ describe functional subject areas that are unique to an organization and represent the lowest levels of data and provide the design foundation for the data warehouse, data marts, applications development, business analysis and strategic planning..
    a. Enterprise Data Models
    b. Template Data Models
    c. Subject Data Models
    d. Business Data Models

EXERCISES

1. Write a brief note on the commonly employed data analysis techniques and their significance.
2. What are Data models? List down three data models with a brief explanation for each.
3. List down the key steps in data modeling along with a brief explanation.
4. Write short notes on the following:
   - Data Marts

- Data Warehousing Life Cycle

5. Enumerate on the structure and composition of a data warehouse.

RESEARCH ACTIVITIES

In continuation to the research activity listed in Chapter 1, you are requested to:

Choose an appropriate data analysis technique and data model with due justification provided for their selection

Prepare a data warehousing life cycle detailing the major phases

---

---

[i] Method for an Integrated Knowledge Environment (MIKE 2.0) is an open source delivery framework for Enterprise Information Management. It provides a common methodology that can be applied across different projects with the Information Management Domain.

CHAPTER 2 - KNOWLEDGE MAP

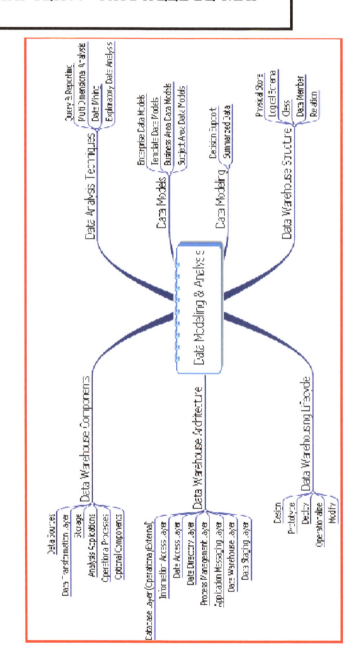

BIBLIOGRAPHY

1. Michael Hahne, Lothar Burow, and Torben Elvers, XML-Datenimport in das SAP Business Information Warehouse bei Bayer MaterialScience, Auf dem Weg zur Integration Factory, 231-251, 2005.

2. D. Calvanese, G. De Giacomo, M. Lenzerini, D. Nardi, and R. Rosati, Source Integration in Data Warehousing, DEXA'98, 192—197, 1998.

3. G. Zhou, R. Hull, R. King, and J.-C. Franchitti, Supporting Data Integration and Warehousing Using H2O, IEEE Data Engineering Bulletin, 18:2, 29-40, 1995.

4. Michael Hahne, Time aspects in SAP Business Information Warehouse, Concurrent Engineering - Enhanced Interoperable Systems, 69-74, 2003.

5. Michael Hahne, Grafische Repräsentation mehrdimensionaler Datenmodelle des SAP Business Information Warehouse, Multikonferenz Wirtschaftsinformatik (MKWI) 2004, 152-166, 2003.

6. Sergio Lujan-Mora and Juan Trujillo, A Comprehensive Method for Data Warehouse Design, DMDW, 2003.

7. Hajer Baazaoui Zghal, Sami Faiz, and Henda Ben Ghezala, CASME: A CASE Tool for Spatial Data Marts Design and Generation, DMDW, 2003.

8. Veronika Peralta and Raul Ruggia, Using Design Guidelines to Improve Data Warehouse Logical Design, DMDW, 2003.

9. Michael Hahne, Logische Datenmodellierung zur Abbildung mehrdimensionaler Datenstrukturen im SAP Business Information Warehouse, BTW, 630-647, 2003.

10. Franck Ravat, Olivier Teste, Ronan Tournier, and Gilles Zurfluh, Finding an application-appropriate model for XML data warehouses, Information Systems, 35:6, 662—687, 2010.

11. J. Gray, H. Schek, M. Stonebraker, and J. Ullman, Lowell Report, 2003.

12. Eva Kuhn, The Zero-Delay Data Warehouse: Mobilizing Heterogeneous Databases, VLDB, 2003.

13. Rob Weir, Taoxin Peng, and Jon Kerridge, Best Practice for Implementing a Data Warehouse: A Review for Strategic Alignment, DMDW, 2003.

14. Surajit Chaudhuri, Umeshwar Dayal, and Venkatesh Ganti, Database technology for decision support systems, IEEE Computer, 48—55, 2001.

15. Surajit Chaudhuri and Umesh Dayal, An Overview of Data Warehousing and OLAP Technology, ACM SIGMOD Record, 26:1, 1997.

16. M.C. Wu and A.P. Buchmann, Research Issues in Data Warehousing, BTW, 1997.

17. Phillip M. Fernandez and Donovan Schneider, The Ins and Outs (and everything in between) of Data Warehousing, ACM SIGMOD, 1996 (SIGMOD membership required).

18. Jennifer Widom, Research Problems in Data Warehousing, Int'l Conf. on Information and Knowledge Management, 1995.

19. Zaker, M., Phon-Amnuaisuk, S., and Haw, S.C., Hierarchical denormalizing: a possibility to optimize the data warehouse design , International Journal of Computer, 2:1, 143—150, 2009.

20. Lars Brumester and Matthias Goeken, Multidimensional reference models for data warehouse development, ICEIS 2007, 2007.

21. Matthias Goeken and Ralf Knacksted, Method for user oriented modelling of data warehouse systems, ICEIS 2006, 2006.

Journals

1. **International Journal of Data Warehousing and Mining (IJDWM)**

   Source URL <http://www.igi-global.com>

2. **Data & Knowledge Engineering**

   Source URL <http://www.sciencedirect.com>

Answers To Multiple Choice Questions

Chapter 1

1. c
2. a
3. a
4. b
5. a
6. a
7. c
8. c
9. a
10. c

Chapter 2

1. b
2. a
3. c
4. a
5. a
6. Time Series Analysis
7. b

8. a

9. d

10. c